For Those Who Grieve
Guidance for interpreting death and offering comfort

compiled by
R. Earl Allen

BROADMAN PRESS
Nashville, Tennessee

© Copyright 1978 • Broadman Press
All rights reserved.

4224-11

ISBN: 0-8054-2411-3

Dewey Decimal Classification: 242.4
Subject heading: CONSOLATION

Library of Congress Catalog Card Number: 77-075558
Printed in the United States of America

Denny J. Wright

For Those Who Grieve

Dedicated
to the
members of the
Southern Baptist Convention
Executive Committee
and to its leaders
Porter W. Routh
Executive Secretary-Treasurer
and
Albert McClellan
Associate Executive Secretary

Preface

I think *Memorial Messages* has been the best received of any of my books as it has gone through five printings. The book was really written for preachers but has been used by all. For Those Who Grieve is written for the laity as well as ministers. I have tried to bring together the thinking of some of our finest preachers.

I am in great debt to my brethren for their great contributions to the book. It is sent forth with a prayer that it may be helpful For Those Who Grieve.

Again, I must thank my associates Gordon Dutile and Randel Trull for the help they gave to me while putting together this book. My deep appreciation to Arline Harris and Barbara Brian for their help with the manuscript.

R. Earl Allen

Contents

Part I	The Individual and Grief	
	1. Ministry to the Dying Person David James Farmer	12
	2. A Testimony of the Bereaved Carl Duck	23
Part II	The Pastor and Grief	
	3. Interpreting Death to Children Wesley R. Monfalcone	32
	4. A Pastor's View of Funerals R. Earl Allen	41
Part III	The Mourners and Grief	
	5. She Is Not Dead Carl E. Bates	50
	6. The Language of Sorrow Charles G. Fuller	53
	7. Not Dead, Just Moved Away Herschel H. Hobbs	58
	8. Victory in Jesus Landrum Leavell	62
	9. The Blessed Dead Jaroy Weber	66
	10. The Good Man Russell H. Dilday, Jr.	69

11.	On Healing Troubled Hearts James L. Pleitz	72
12.	Our Eternal Home W. Randall Lolley	76
13.	The Hope of Seeing Jesus James W. Bryant	80
14.	The Way Paul Looked at Death Walter G. Nunn	86
15.	The Hands of Death Are Beautiful R. Y. Bradford	90
16.	Slipping the Bonds of Earth Mahan Siler, Jr.	93
17.	What Is the Color of Death? W. Ches Smith, III	95
18.	When Is a Man Ready to Die? Richard Jackson	98
19.	Not Why, But How Charles E. Harvey	103
20.	I Believe in Immortality James P. Wesberry	107
21.	A Choice of Death Jack P. Lowndes	114
22.	Graveside Committal Service Charles G. Fuller	118
23.	Military Graveside Service Francis Jackson Redford	120

Part IV The Bible and Grief

24.	Thoughts About Death W. O. Vaught, Jr.	124

Contributing Authors   135

Part I

The Individual and Grief

1.
Ministry to the Dying Person
David James Farmer

Would the following introduction catch your attention?

> For a time it seemed as though we in America had almost succeeded in eliminating from the modern vocabulary that horribly distasteful word death and its equally offensive counterpart, "dying." To be certain, we were bombarded constantly with reports of mass starvations, highway mayhem, political assassinations, and even color-televised war. But these events were far away and unrelated to our everyday lives.
>
> Oh, it is true that we all suffered the loss of a loved one or friend during this period; but usually they were thoughtful enough to "pass on" in a hospital or nursing home, certainly not in our own homes. And so we almost made "death" obscene and "dying" un-American.
>
> But what went wrong? Well, as always in ventures of this type, there are some busybodies around to mess things up. There was that Dr. Kübler-Ross in Chicago who actually had the nerve to ask dying patients about the way they thought things were going. And there was Evelyn Waugh and his most disrespectful book, The Loved One. Imagine making fun of "Slumber Rooms" and "Perpetual Rest" cemeteries! In addition to these radicals, there was a growing number of doctors, nurses, ministers, family members, and dying persons themselves who became increasingly disturbed with our efforts to rid the language of those most distressing words.
>
> Well, we may not have been totally successful in banning death and dying from everybody's conversation; but, for those of us in polite society, we shall only "pass on" after having "remained guarded."

MINISTRY TO THE DYING PERSON

I have been deliberately facetious in order to illustrate an important social phenomenon, the recent attempts to reverse the death-denying tendencies of our culture. Not only the minister, but also the layman, needs to be acquainted with some of the developments in this area. I offer you some concrete suggestions as you seek to exercise your calling to serve the church by helping dying persons.

The Christian church has always stood for the frank assertion that death is part of being human. We cannot look at the life of Jesus without acknowledging his death, his burial, and his resurrection. To do so would prevent us from ever knowing the gospel of resurrection. [1] Because of the significance of the resurrection, we in the household of faith should welcome the efforts which help us to face death and dying more realistically and humanely. In fact, the Christian faith offers much to their efforts just as it stands to gain much in return.

I am particularly interested in sharing with you some ideas on how you can help provide Christian love to dying persons both in and out of your local church fellowship. Your role as servant gives you a great opportunity not only to be a friend to those who are dying but to represent to them the One who himself died and who conquered death. I shall first summarize the basic needs of the terminally-ill hospital patient (since most persons die in the hospital), and then offer some specific suggestions about how you can go about meeting these needs.

What are the needs of the dying person?

1. A dying person needs to be able to have a feeling of complete faith and confidence in his personal physician and the hospital staff who care for him. The person needs to be able to believe that everything possible is being done to meet his medical and nursing needs. This may involve working to cure the illness or simply striving to relieve as much pain and discomfort as possible. In any case, the patient needs to feel that everything possible is

being done for him and, until the very end, that there is some hope for recovery.

2. He needs to know that the ones who matter most to him still love and care for him even though he is in the process of leaving them. This is particularly true in regard to one's immediate family and close friends. Needless to say, the persons who determine whether or not these needs are met are themselves experiencing grief as they struggle to give up their loved ones.

3. The dying person needs also to be in a position to rest assured that those dependent upon him will have their needs met when he is gone. This is particularly true regarding fathers and mothers of dependent children. I have known several dying persons who were far more concerned with the needs of their survivors than with their own dying.

4. A person has intense emotional needs as he faces his own death. Kübler-Ross identifies these needs in terms of five distinct stages through which a dying person passes. [2]

Denial means that a person takes time to adjust to the diagnosis that he is terminally ill by denying the reality of the diagnosis. This is a normal reaction to a shocking situation. Within appropriate bounds, it is an emotionally necessary response.

Anger means that a person can no longer totally deny his condition and that he needs the acceptance of others in order to ventilate his normal feelings of anger, frustration, fear, helplessness, and disappointment at the prospect of dying.

Bargaining means that a person slowly realizes that his protests are to no avail and that the certainty of his death cannot be avoided. During this stage, he may seek to negotiate with his doctor or with God for more time in return for certain changes in his life.

Depression means that the person begins to realize that no bargains can be made and that he is going to die. At this point, he begins to accept death both intellectually and emotionally. He begins to mourn the loss of loved ones, accustomed habits, and all the other increasingly beautiful and lovely dimensions of being alive.

Acceptance means that the person has all but separated himself from the land of the living and is ready to affirm his destiny as a mortal creature.

A person may not pass through all of these stages to reach the point of acceptance, but most persons need to pass through the first four in order to reach the last. And certainly not everyone goes beyond the first stage. Every doctor and pastor knows of people who go to their graves denying that anything is the matter with them. And the same goes for persons who die in a state of anger, bargaining, or depression.

Many factors shape how "successful" one is in his dying: his own basic personality structure, the cultural tendencies to deny death, the amount of time a person has to die (accident victims, for example, may not have the time to pass through any of the stages), whether or not the doctor has told the person of his condition, and his basic emotional and spiritual health at that time in his life.

In addition to these factors, there is one other essential variable: Does the dying person have at least one person with whom he can maintain an emotionally honest relationship? The dying person needs to have the freedom to share any feeling, no matter how negative, with at least one other person. This trusted friend may be his doctor, nurse, pastor, spouse, or friend; but without at least one such relationship it is virtually impossible for a dying person to end his life in peace or with dignity. He may never choose to confide his fears, but the dying person needs to feel that he *could* if he so desired.

5. Most persons who reach the emotional stage of acceptance do so because they have genuine moral and spiritual resources. For many, these resources are supplied by religious faith and by

their particular faith community. For others, these resources are supplied by their own personal creed or philosophy of life. In any case, dying persons need and want to approach death with a feeling of being at peace with themselves, with others, and with God. They need to feel that their life has been a good one. They need to feel that they are not carrying to their graves any fundamental regrets or unforgiven sins. They need to feel that their lives end with a certain wholeness and with a certain completion.

The need to die with integrity is one of life's basic developmental tasks, according to Erik Erikson.[3] In Christian terms, this is described as needing and wanting to die *in a state of grace* as opposed to dying *in a state of sin*. We may say that dying with integrity is a spiritual dimension of facing one's death.

Now that we have summarized the basic needs of the dying patient to face death with dignity, what are some ways that concerned laymen can help? First, I suggest that you commit yourself to preparation and cooperation. There is strength in numbers and better results with leadership. You may want to initiate such a ministry by a seminar on "Ministering to the Dying." Each participant would need to read Kübler-Ross' *On Death and Dying* beforehand. Then either Kübler-Ross' film, *Until I Die,* or Broadman's excellent film, *Though I Walk Through the Valley,* [4] should be scheduled. At the beginning of the seminar, the leader would give a brief lecture followed by one or both of the films. Then the meeting would be opened up for discussion and questions.

The participants need to share their feeling honestly about death and dying if the seminar is to be a success. Participants need to share their feelings about visiting dying patients. If after the seminar, the group is still committed to this special ministry the pastor or another skilled person should coordinate their efforts. One possible way to begin is to visit the hospital with another pastor or experienced layman. This approach provides for individual preparation, group support, and leadership. Beyond this each should seek the blessings of Almighty God as he approaches his mission: "Who can approach such a task with anything less than the whole of heaven's host behind him?" [5]

Now, let me offer some concrete suggestions about caring for dying persons. The first need of the dying patient is the ability to have complete trust in his doctor and in the hospital staff. The church has little control over this factor. Fortunately, in the vast majority of cases, concern is not necessary. However, there are a few ways you can help a patient to trust his doctor and the hospital staff. You can acquaint yourself with the fundamental do's and don'ts of general hospital visitation. I suggest that you read Chaplain Bill Justice's helpful handbook, *Don't Sit on the Bed,* [6] or ask someone more experienced to help you to develop your skills in hospital visitation. Guidelines which I consider to be crucial are:

1. Always introduce yourself to either the family or the charge-nurse before visiting a dying person. They can give you invaluable information regarding his condition as well as introducing you to the patient if you do not already know the person.

2. Watch for "isolation" or "no visitors" signs; they have a purpose and should be respected.

3. If you are unable to call on a patient for any reason after having arrived at the hospital, leave a note with the family or the nurse. For a person not able to receive visitors, notes, cards, or small gifts are most welcomed.

4. Introduce yourself very clearly since patients encounter several strangers every day.

5. Seek to be as relaxed as possible. Find a seat near the patient so that he may see you comfortably.

6. Watch out for tubes, needles, oxygen equipment, and so forth and avoid contact with them.

7. Be prepared to see a person with changed physical features, such as changes in weight and color. Try not to show your natural feelings of shock, disgust, or fear at the strange equipment or changes in the patient's appearance.

8. Do not whisper in the room to others. Sick persons are very concerned about not being let in on the truth.

9. Always seek to promote the patient's confidence in the medical and nursing staff. If he is angry at them, listen, but do not criticize them. Do not in any way impair the patient's trust in those whom he needs very much.

10. Pay attention to the time so that you do not visit overly long with a seriously ill person.

These are only a few of the many factors involved in a successful hospital call, but all such considerations are based on concern for the patient and on common sense.

The second need of the dying person is reassurance that those who matter most to him still love him. By the fact that you come to visit, you are saying that you care, that the church cares, and that God cares. It is hard for us to imagine how much one short visit can mean to a sick person. It is impossible for us to imagine what it can mean to a dying person.

Mrs. Kate Woolley, a friend of mine, has shared some of the ways friends cared for her husband, Davis, when he was dying. She impressed on me how much simple cards and short visits meant to her husband. She reminded me about how important it is not to delay in expressing appreciation to a dying person. Do not wait until it is too late to buy flowers or gifts: "Give your gifts while the person can enjoy them: Be extravagant at a time when he can receive your love! Remember the woman who anointed the feet of Jesus with expensive perfume and how Jesus appreciated her concern for Him *before* He died." [7]

Remind the patient that his affections and talents are still needed by those who are well because he still has the need to be needed like everyone else. Use good judgment in spacing your visits over a period of time instead of coming only at the beginning of the illness or near its end. Try to develop a relationship with a seriously ill person before he begins to separate himself from others. When he begins to do that, you may be too late.

The third basic need of the dying person is assurance that his or her family will be taken care of. Because of the need for good communication, the place for someone in the church to coordinate assistance is obvious. Many things may be done. Here are a few suggestions. Be willing to listen to and help with the patient's concern about family finances and other matters if he so chooses to discuss them. Help the family with chores such as shopping, child care, and other family business. Offer to stay with the patient so that the family can rest and attend to other personal matters. Be careful to listen to and take seriously the family's feelings of anxiety, exhaustion, anger, and grief. A caring fellowship such as a concerned and thoughtful church goes a long way in helping to provide peace of mind for a dying person who is naturally anxious about the welfare of his loved ones.

The fourth area of need with which the dying person is confronted is that of acute emotional stress. Here is where he needs an emotionally honest relationship with at least one other person. Generally, a person's pastor or doctor provides this relationship. Oftentimes, the immediate family is too caught up in its feelings to be able to give what the relationship demands: complete acceptance. If some other person is providing that relationship, then your role may be that of a supportive friend. However, the patient may not have anyone with whom he is comfortable enough to confide his feelings and he chose you to be his confidant. If he chooses you, you have received a great honor and an even greater responsibility. To fulfill this responsibility, you need to be aware of your own feelings in regard to death and to be reasonably able to accept them. (We cannot accept in others what we cannot accept in ourselves.)

At whatever level you relate to a dying person, it is helpful to try to assess his emotional state at the given time. Use Kübler-Ross' five stages to do this. If the person is *denying* his condition, do not interfere. He has that freedom, and besides, no person can hold before himself constantly the fact that he is dying.

If the person expresses *anger,* even at the ones he loves the most, allow him the freedom to do so without judgment. He is in all probability ventilating his frustrations and fears. Listening is appropriate here.

If the person is in the stage of *bargaining,* allow him the privilege to do so. Trying to convince him that God does not make deals will do no good. The dying person will arrive at that conclusion soon enough.

If the patient is *depressed,* be generous with your support without being superficial or insensitive to the patient's feelings. "Cheer up, everything is OK!" is best left unsaid. Saying, "I care that you are sad. Would you like to talk with me about it?" is usually a great help. Also this would be the time for gifts and cards. It is a time to request something the patient can give. For example, "John, tell me about that cabinet you made. I admire it and would like to try to make one like it myself." This feeds the person's self-esteem, something which each of us always needs.

If the person has come to *accept* the reality of his dying, he may not need to say very much. Your silent presence may be all that is necessary. Here, physical touch is deeply meaningful. Silence and touch express feelings too deep for words. It is important to realize that as death approaches the person separates himself emotionally from everyone, even those who matter most to him. Unless you are particularly close to the person, you should allow the patient's family and pastor to have the final conscious opportunities for visiting him. The approach of death is the time for your

MINISTRY TO THE DYING PERSON

support of the ones suffering the loss of the person.

The final needs of the dying which I discussed concerned spiritual matters. Normally, a person will depend upon a clergyman for spiritual care as he faces death. If the person you visit is not acquainted with a minister, you can render an invaluable service by introducing him to your pastor, the hospital chaplain, or to a clergyman whom the patient chooses. This does not mean that laymen should avoid meeting the spiritual needs of the sick and dying. Laymen can offer to pray with the person, promise to remember him in their private prayers as well as in the church's prayers of intercession, and read the Bible to him.

By doing these things, you strengthen what faith the person already has. Many times a person needs to confess to someone a heretofore hidden sin. If a person so confesses to you, listen to him and take his guilt seriously. Assure him of your absolute intention to keep the confession a secret. After the confession, assure him of your forgiveness and God's. If you do not feel it is appropriate or possible for you to hear such a confession, by all means seek out a pastor who can and introduce him to the patient.

Remember, all that you do as a representative of Christ and of your church is a spiritual ministry. If you simply listen to a dying person as he tells of his past fishing trips which he loved so much, or if you help feed someone who cannot feed himself, you are a part of God's presence with that person.

The question arises at this point about the person who is not a Christian. I believe a dying person has the right to bring this subject up himself just as Jesus allowed the dying thieves on the crosses next to him to make their own decisions. If the person asks you about your faith, chances are he is convinced about the authenticity of your concern for him as well as the authenticity of your relationship to God. If he asks, you are in a better position to bear witness to your faith.

I suggest private prayer for the person and a faithful witness in deed as well as in word as the best approaches toward a non-Christian. In no case do I recommend forcing a dying person to face this (or any other issue) without having first consulted with the person's family and his physician.

---

[1] Elisabeth Kübler-Ross, M. D., *On Death and Dying* (New York: The Macmillan Company, 1969), pp. 38–137.

[2] Erik Erikson, *Childhood and Society* (New York: W. W. Norton and Company, 1951), pp. 231–33.

[3] *Until I Die* is a film on the work of Elisabeth Kübler-Ross and produced by Video-Nursing of Evanston, Illinois. *Though I Walk Through the Valley* is a real-life documentary of a dying man and his family and is produced by Broadman Films of Nashville, Tennessee. I suggest the first for its psychological instruction and the second for its realistic portrayal of the religious and personal dimensions of dying.

[4] Richard C. Cabot and Russell L. Dicks, *The Art of Ministering to the Sick* (New York: The Macmillan Company, 1944), p. 61.

[5] William G. Justice, *Don't Sit on the Bed!* (Nashville: Broadman Press, 1973).

[6] Kate Wilkins Woolley, "Care During Terminal Illness," *The Journal of Pastoral Care,* Vol. XXVI. (Kutztown, Pa.: The Association for Clinical Pastoral Education, June, 1972), p. 118.

[7] Carl J. Scherzer, *Ministering to the Dying* (Englewood Cliffs, New Jersey: Prentice-Hall, 1963). This small volume is an excellent guide to ministering to the spiritual needs of the dying.

[EDITOR'S NOTE: This chapter is from *Proclaim*. © Copyright 1972, The Sunday School Board of the Southern Baptist Convention. All rights reserved. Used by permission.]

2.
A Testimony of the Bereaved
Carl Duck

(Sunday morning message following the tragic, accidental death of the pastor's only son at age twenty-four.)

Blessed be God, even the Father of our Lord Jesus Christ, the Father of mercies, and the God of all comfort; who comforteth us in all our tribulation, that we may be able to comfort them who are in any trouble, by the comfort wherewith we ourselves are comforted of God. For as the sufferings of Christ abound in us, so our consolation also aboundeth by Christ (2 Cor. 1:3–5).

"So our consolation also aboundeth by Christ," Paul declared. And Christ had promised, "My grace is sufficient for thee" (2 Cor. 12:9).

Friends, my message today will be more a testimony than a sermon. I hope you will understand. I feel that a congregation of people as loving and as dear and as precious as you are deserves to hear what a pastor feels and what a pastor and his family experience in time of great sorrow. As I bare my heart to you, I ask, above all, that you please pray for me.

You have heard me say, from this pulpit in worship services, in funeral messages, and in so many other times and places, that God provides for his own. Today I want to bear testimony to you, my people, of the truthfulness of what I have said to you through the years. As I share my testimony with you today, it really is the testimony of my wife and myself that God does provide.

First, there are two thoughts I want to press to your hearts. I want to say to you that the sorrow through which we've passed has been the most difficult thing that we've ever experienced. You can well imagine that. We do not understand what has happened. And being as human as anybody else, we have asked over and over again, "Why?" We've had our questions and our doubts. We've had a deep, deep hurt, a scar that will abide in our lives and in our home until the end. We have wept, and we shall weep for years to come. But whatever I'm going to say today, it is said out of a background of being the most human pastor that you could possibly ever know.

The other thing I want to say is this. My wife and I are perfectly willing for God's will to be done in all that has happened. A long time before our son was born, we gave him to God. We prayed that God's will would be done in his birth; through the years we've prayed that God's will would be done in his life. And because we gave our son to God's will we are now prepared to say in his death, "Thy will be done." To the best of our ability we've done that, and in it we have found peace.

Now I share with you our testimony of assurance in the hope that it will encourage you and in some way prepare you for whatever you must meet in your own life and the sorrow you may have to bear along the way. And I repeat, I do so out of a deep burden of conviction that this is what God would have me do. Here are the five things that I share with you that come out of our hearts from our experience.

I. We bear witness to the sufficiency of God's grace.

We want to bear witness to the congregation that when life's greatest sorrow comes, God's grace is sufficient. Now please write this down in your hearts and hear me today as you've never heard me before in the ten years that I've been preaching in your pulpit. From experience—bitter, hard, hurting, crushing experience—I want to say to you today with more conviction than ever before that whatever you must face in your life, whatever sorrow comes your way, whatever you must bear in your home and in your family, God's grace will see you through it if you will trust in him.

Were it not for the grace of God, and in a real sense of hope because of a living, personal faith in Christ, I am here to say to you that one could not stand the hurt of losing a child. God's grace is sufficient, and to that I bear glad testimony today.

God said, "As one whom his mother comforteth, so will I comfort you" (Isa. 66:13). And in Psalms we read: "As a father pitieth his children, so the Lord pitieth them that fear him"(103:13). "Come unto me, all ye that labour and are heavy laden, Jesus said, "and I will give you rest" (Matt. 11:28).

I want you to know that the grace of God is sufficient to see you through whatever trouble you ever have in your life. If trouble should knock at the door of your house today and sorrow were to be your lot, if your heart is not filled with the comforting peace of God's grace, then what are you going to trust and upon what will you lean? Let me tell you from my heart and with all my soul, there is absolutely no way for another to describe how comforting and wonderful and peaceful is the grace of God when the terrible and tragic news of sorrow comes. God's grace is sufficient!

II. We bear witness to the sustaining strength of Christian friends.

On Wednesday night in the prayer service I said to the people that I have never seen Christian love showered so abundantly upon a family as in these days. You have surrounded our family with your love; you have taken us to God in prayer. You have said, "When you hurt, we hurt!" You have, by your example and your acts, preached the greatest sermon on Christian love that I have ever seen. And I'm here today to bear witness to the sustaining strength that comes through Christian friends. Oh, how we need each other! What a blessing it is to have friends who stand by your side and hold up your hands and pray for you when your heart is broken. We shall be grateful to you forever for the way you have seen us through our sorrow.

Dear friends, let me tell you that the greatest thing in earthly relationships is the love of your friends when you come to the deep waters. That's the reason I keep encouraging you to be active in the church, to put your life into the service of God with other Christians, and to let your friends be the friends of God. For when you come to the time your strength is no more and you're up against a wall you can't go over or around and your whole world comes tumbling in, then your Christian friends come and put their arms of love about you and they see you through.

I want to ask you today if you're not active in the church, if you do not have God's people as your dearest friends then do something about it. Get busy, cultivate the friends of God as your friends, for there will come a day when you're going to need them. The folks who really know how to help are the folks who love God. Our church is full of the greatest people of Christian love I've ever seen in my life, and I thank you for it.

III. We bear witness to the surpassing value of family love.

Now here is what I mean: the greatest thing that you can have in your family is a sure and deep and abiding love for one another. It is because we shared in our family that kind of love that I can say to you that every memory we have of every experience through which we passed is a happy memory. And I want to ask you dads, are you sure your boys know that you love them? Mothers, be sure your children know that you love them. Children, don't you let a day pass by but that you let your parents know you love them.

Now please permit me a more personal word here. We shared in our family a love between the three of us that ran so deep and was so meaningful that we shall carry on until the Lord comes or until he calls us home. Then we will see our son again in the assurance that all through those twenty-four years and six months we loved each other. Thank God we did! I do not believe I could stand here nor could I go on if I did not have the assurance in my heart that we loved one another.

Some of you may not have shared with your children how much you love them in a long, long time. And some of you children have not told your parents that you love them in a long, long time. God forbid that should be! I pray that none of you will have to go through the sorrow we've known; but if it should happen, and you lost one of yours, would you live in the nagging regret that you didn't love as you should? God wants our families to be families where there is love; in everything we share and do, that love should reign supreme in our families. Oh, dear parents, love your children! Love them into the kingdom of God and love them without any shame. Share that love and let them know that love and you'll be thankful ten thousand times!

IV. We bear witness to the supreme importance of every young person living for the Lord.

Now, young people, let me speak to your hearts. I stand before you today as a father who has lost his son, and I beg you, plead with you: Give your life to the Lord! Trust him now; live for God! And whether your life be short or long, if you've given it to the Lord and your influence counts for him, you will be blessed forever.

The Bible says, "Remember now thy Creator in the days of thy youth" (Eccl. 12:1).

I remember, and oh, how I shall go on remembering, that wonderful night when my little eight-year-old boy told me that the Lord was speaking to his heart and he wanted to be saved. There in our living room he gave his heart to Jesus, and with these hands I baptized him.

Young people, give your life to the Lord and do it now. Live for him and let your influence be counted for him. Don't wait! The Bible says, "Boast not thyself of tomorrow; for thou knowest not what a day may bring forth" (Prov. 27:1).

I bear sad testimony to you today, that's right! And so if you've been waiting, young man, give your life to the Lord today. If you have a child that is unsaved, parents, don't let this day close until you talk to him about Jesus. Don't let your children take a chance on eternity without God. I'm so glad, I'm so very glad my son was saved!

V. We bear witness to the surety of our hope in Jesus Christ.

It is so wonderful that Jesus conquered death! He has given to us eternal life and because he lives, we shall live also. The hope of eternal life is brighter in my heart today than it's ever been. One day Jesus Christ is coming again. We're going to be gathered together with him and our loved ones on that shore, that beautiful place where there is no death, no sorrow, no separation, and where together we shall sing and praise and serve the name of Jesus forever.

If you do not have that hope in Jesus Christ, you are the poorest and the most miserable person in this earth—I don't care what else you have to hold in your hands! The greatest thing you can have, the greatest assurance you can possess, the greatest joy you will ever know, the greatest peace you can ever have is what you have in the Lord Jesus Christ. And he is real!

When we came back from the grave where we had placed the body of our dear son, I said to my Bonnie, "Isn't it wonderful that this is not the end! In God's own time, we shall have him again." And, thank God, when we do not understand, it's so peaceful to leave it in God's hands.

Now I've tried so falteringly to share with you my testimony because I believe you deserve to know what your pastor feels. There is no way for me to tell you how difficult it has been for me today, but I thank you for your prayers.

I close with this. It's not what I feel that is so important, it's what I know; and it's all because of Jesus Christ! I want to preach with more effectiveness and power than ever before in my life, and I want to give myself anew to my Lord today. Will you join me in doing that, for Jesus' sake? For Jesus' sake!

Part II

The Pastor and Grief

3.
Interpreting Death to Children
Wesley R. Monfalcone

Most of us have trouble dealing with death.

Some years ago, before our own children were born, my wife and I "house-sat" for some friends while they were on vacation. The only pet in the family was a small turtle owned by the eleven-year-old boy. To our dismay, the turtle died that week. We rushed out and bought another just like it, hoping Carl would not notice the difference and never know of his pet's death. To our surprise, we discovered when the family returned that Carl had tired of the turtle and the parents were hoping it would soon die of old age!

Our reluctance to deal with death in relation to children may create difficulties in more serious situations. Recently a twelve-year-old boy (we'll call him John) was admitted to Louisville General Hospital with injuries from the collision of his family's pickup truck and a tractor-trailer truck. John's parents were killed in the accident.

The family was very reluctant to tell John of his parents' death immediately, feeling they should wait until he was physically better and until the "right" family member could find the "right" moment. For three days family members and other friends who visited John avoided discussion of the accident or his parents and gingerly sidestepped questions about them. Finally a grandmother, two aunts, an uncle, the ward nurse, and the hospital chaplain gathered to tell John. While they waited for him to have his bandage changed in another room, a doctor simply and calmly told John about his parents. Not only did the little drama fall flat but the tragedy was also that for three days John was deprived of supportive care and an opportunity to begin working through his grief because family members were so anxious that they were unable to share reality with him.

We usually try to keep death far from children. We feel that they are insensitive and do not know what happens around them or, on the other hand, that they are supersensitive and extremely fragile. Because of our own anxiety about death, we ignore the fact that children are aware of most of what happens around them, especially regarding changed relationships and emotion-charged events.

We forget, too, that death permeates life. The child is exposed very early to dead bugs and, perhaps, to dead pets. He sees literally hundreds of artificial deaths on television. Though he is likely to be kept isolated from it, it is probable that death will occur to a person he knows while he is a child, or at least before he grows out of adolescence.

Death raises thorny questions for parents and others who care for children. How can one prepare a child for the eventuality of encountering death? What may we say when probing questions are asked? How does one deal with an embarrassing situation, as when a five-year-old, told Grandma is sick, asks, "Are you going to die, Grandma?"

Preparing Children to Deal with Death

One who wants to help children prepare to deal with death must begin with his own feelings and attitudes. This is difficult in a society which tries to isolate death. We hide the dying in hospitals and nursing homes and try to cover repulsive aspects of death in funeral homes. Now that many inhibitions about sex have been discarded, some say that death is the new obscenity and the language of death the new pornography.[1]

One sign of contemporary change in that attitude is the deep interest of many professionals in the subject. A body of literature has grown up dealing with death and dying from every perspective. Some are now calling for death education geared to the interests and needs of each age group. The adult who wants to help children deal with death can prepare himself by reading some of this literature and sharing his own feelings about death with others. A study of biblical attitudes toward death may be a good beginning for a group.

There are many occasions for the sensitive, listening adult to help a child deal with death. "Artificial" deaths provide these opportunities. Many children see literally hundreds of staged deaths on television before they enter the first grade. Many children's stories involve death or some life-threatening situations. Although parents may cringe at Gretel pushing the wicked witch into the hot oven and at the stepmother poisoning Snow White, at least one authority on children says these are helpful. They help children learn on the fantasy level to cope with fears, and they provide reassurance that these fantasized terrors are unreal.[2] In any case, they may raise questions that are occasions for teaching about death.

The death of a pet can be a good learning experience. All sorts of questions may arise as a child is confronted with a beloved dog who no longer moves and plays, who does not come when called, and who must be disposed of rather quickly. Some sort of "funeral" gives children an opportunity to act out feelings and fears and to put the experience behind them.

Finally, one may help a child in the experience of the death of a person. This is especially true if it is not a person upon whom the child depends for most of his emotional support. When an elderly woman who was a good friend of our family died, our four-year-old had many questions about her. My wife offered to take Mark to see "Aunt" Bess in the funeral home. They went in the afternoon when very few people were there. Mark was able to see the body, see some people who had come because they loved her, and ask questions about the whole situation.

In this low-key experience Mark learned something about death and had a chance to say his good-bye to "Aunt" Bess. Later feedback indicated this was a positive experience; it helped Mark voice some of his questions and fears and left openings for him to raise new questions.

The death of a person the child knows is an opportunity to share our Christian faith and beliefs. At the level of the child's understanding, we may share our trust in God, our hope in his constant presence, and our belief in resurrection and eternal life.

Children's Ages and Understandings of Death

How may one help prepare a particular child to deal with death? Many adults are stumped by lack of knowledge of the levels of understanding and feeling of different age children. The two-year-old requires different concepts and methods of communication from the five- or ten-year-old. Studies of children help us understand the normal developmental differences in their thinking and feeling. Among those who have investigated children's attitudes toward death, the work of Maria Nagy and Sylvia Anthony in the 1940s is basic, for their conclusions have been confirmed by later researchers.[3] Following is an outline of the attitudes and capabilities of various age groups in regard to death.

Birth to Two Years

The child in the first two years of life has no real understanding of death. But although the concept is beyond him, he does have experiences and behaviors related to death. *Separation* is the most significant aspect of death for the infant. If his mother figure is taken from him, he will go through a "grief" experience, including protest, despair, and detachment.[4] Hopefully, he will find another mother figure to whom he may attach himself.

From Three to Five

Children in this age range have many questions (spoken and unspoken) about death. As they are curious about the rest of their world, they are curious about dead bugs, pets, and people. To these children death is reversible. In their play, the dead may immediately be able to eat and walk again. They do not conceptualize death as a final event. *Separation* is still the most significant aspect of their concept of death. When a parent dies, for instance, one of the child's first thoughts is, Who will take care of me now?

From Five to Nine

From age five onward, the child gradually begins to understand that death is *final and inevitable*. These children have a strong tendency to personify death. Death is a person in horrible clothing or a skeleton who comes and takes people away. By age nine or ten a child has developed sufficient mental powers and emotional security to acknowledge death as a biological fact which comes to everyone. At this point the child is capable of expressing sorrow, a capacity which deepens through adolescence. Younger children are capable of only fleeting feelings of sadness; these are much more transitory than the grief of their elders. Children up to about age nine are far more deeply affected by the reactions of others to a death than by internal grief.

As with other developmental tasks, individual children differ in the speed with which they arrive at these levels of understanding. Some children may express concepts of death and experience emotions related to it that are beyond, or behind, the stages outlined for their age. The categories are helpful as suggestions of the intellectual and feeling content a child may be able to handle.

Two important conclusions may be drawn from this kind of developmental outline. First, children do think about death and are affected by it. Second, it is as unfair to a child to expect him to be mature beyond his years in relation to death as it is to force him to be precocious in any other developmental task.

Helping Children Through Grief

We have noted that children, even in infancy, do have grief reactions. How may one help a child through the experience of the death of a person close to him—parent, sibling, grandparent, or friend? The task is immensely significant, for some studies indicate that children who lose a parent or sibling are more prone to delinquent behavior and mental disturbances.[5]

Honesty is important in dealing with children. A child need not know all the facts; information should be geared to his level of understanding. But when an adult refuses to face reality with a child—to face the fact that this person has died, that he will be no more with us, that we are sad about losing him—it sets the stage for mistrust and misunderstanding.

Some explanations given to children are harmful in the long run. "Mama has gone away on a long journey." A child may then reasonably expect her to come back. When she does not, he may become hostile that she has abandoned him without saying good-bye.

"Jesus took her." Jesus may then be seen by the child as a hateful, hostile person who snatches away loved ones without warning or good reason.

"God knew your daddy was good and needed him in heaven." Is that what happens to good people? the child may reason. This explanation provides scant incentive to improve one's behavior.

"He is asleep." This explanation has resulted in sleep problems for many children who feel if they go to sleep they, too, may never awaken.

Simple, honest explanations are imperative. For example, an adult who is a Christian will want to get across the message, "Your daddy died. He will not be with us any more. That makes us very sad because we loved him, and we will miss him. We don't know all the reasons why this happened, but we do believe he is with God now. And now that he is gone, we will take care of you."

Should a child attend the funeral? *Certainly.* It may be very helpful to him, unless he refuses to go or unless there will likely be some bizarre and frightening behavior by adults who attend.

Rituals are important to children. Notice how in their play they often mimic or invent ceremonies. It gives them a chance to learn about their world and to express symbolically what they are not yet able to verbalize.

A child is an important part of a family and should be permitted to participate in all significant family events. A funeral surely qualifies as significant. If he is kept at home by well-meaning adults trying to shield him, the child is deprived of a sense of belonging. He may interpret this as punishment and feel he is somehow responsible for the death.

There are real benefits for the child who attends a funeral. He can recognize more clearly that death has occurred. He can see that others are experiencing the loss, too. He may receive comfort, support, and expressions of love from relatives and friends who are not usually so demonstrative. And he may be reassured that he was not responsible for the death.[6]

The best gift an adult can give a child in grief is understanding and sensitivity. A child needs someone who will *listen*—listen to fears and fantasies and questions. For example, normal children get angry at times and think or say, "I wish you were dead." When in fact that person does die, the child may believe his thoughts and words caused the death. A child always needs the reassurance, "You did not cause him to die." The listening adult will also be sensitive to the deep fear of abandonment that children have and give the reassurance, "You will be taken care of."

The sensitive adult will look for signs of pathological grief—*prolonged* withdrawal, preoccupation, or regression; *prolonged* indifference to friends and schoolwork; *prolonged* eating and drinking problems—and will seek appropriate professional help in these instances.

Helping a Child Face His Own Death

Any consideration of children and death should at least acknowledge the need for helping a child face his own death. Until recently we were able to ignore this task, feeling that children are unaware of approaching death and have no resources with which to confront such a deep and frightening event. Recent investigation has shown, however, that most children have some premonition that death is approaching. Like many dying adults, they often are more able to face this fact than their families. They play the game of ignorance to protect family members who seem unable to deal with the difficult reality.

Physicians, nurses, hospital chaplains, social workers, and others have become interested in this problem. In the next few years there will probably be more extensive research into the difficulties of children facing their own deaths.

Summary

We may prepare ourselves to interpret death to children by first dealing with our own feelings about death and dying. We may recognize that children, too, think and feel and fantasize about death. We may educate ourselves regarding the developmental growth of concepts and feelings regarding death. And we may strive to become caring, sensitive people by listening closely to children and being especially available in times of grief.

We have a rich resource for helping children know the fullness of life and the meaning of death, for though we grieve deeply for those lost to us by death, we do "not grieve as others do who have no hope" (1 Thess. 4:13, RSV).

For the person who wants to read further, the following sources are suggested:

GROLLMAN, EARL A., ed. *Explaining Death to Children.* Boston: Beacon, 1969. (Paper)

JACKSON, EDGAR N. *Telling a Child About Death.* New York: Hawthorn, 1965.

SHERRILL, LEWIS J. AND HELEN H. *Interpreting Death to Children.* Division of Christian Education, National Council of Churches, New York, 1965. (Pamphlet)

---

[1] Richard W. Doss, "Developing a Theology of Death: The Dilemma of the Contemporary Minister," *Foundations,* 14, 3, July-September, 1971, p. 224.

[2] Hella Moller, "Death: Handling the Subject and Affected Students in the Schools," *Explaining Death to Children,* Earl Grollman, ed. (Boston: Beacon, 1967), p. 149.

[3] Maria Nagy, "The Child's View of Death," *The Meaning of Death,* Herman Feifel, ed. (New York: McGraw-Hill, 1959), pp. 49–98. Sylvia Anthony, *The Child's Discovery of Death: A Study in Child Psychology* (New York: Harcourt, Brace, 1940).

[4] Sula Wolff, *Children Under Stress* (Baltimore Penguin Press, 1969), p. 87.

[5] David M. Moriarty, ed., *The Loss of Loved Ones: The Effect of a Death in the Family on Personality Development* (Springfield, Ill.: C. C. Thomas, 1967).

[6] Robert Fulton, "On the Dying of Death," *Explaining Death to Children,* Earl A. Grollman, ed. (Boston: Beacon, 1967) p. 47.

[EDITOR'S NOTE: This chapter is from *The Deacon.* © Copyright 1974, The Sunday School Board of the Southern Baptist Convention. All rights reserved. Used by permission.]

4.
A Pastor's View of Funerals
R. Earl Allen

The death of a loved one is something everyone must face. Many important decisions have to be made when those who are bereaved are unable to think clearly. Often they turn to their pastors or funeral directors for help.

"Death is far too personal to be a private affair," someone has said. Death is an event that impinges on the life of the community. It is an occasion that demands a physician, sometimes a coroner, often an autopsy, and always a certification of death. A mortician, a minister, and friends are needed by those who are left.

Burial rites seem to have been practiced from the very beginning of time, even though there is nothing in the law of Moses that demanded certain burial rituals. Death rites and ceremonies have been instinctive in the social structure of mankind.

Since death is terminal, the rules of health demand that some disposition be made of the body. There are three ways this can be done.

One method, new in our day, is freezing. Some people are having this done today in the hope that future scientists may find some way to bring the body back to life. This is totally unbiblical. After death, there is no chance of bringing life to this earthly body again.

The second method is cremation, which has been frequently used in older areas of the world. This method of disposing of the body is likely to be used more and more, especially in our large cities, because of the growing scarcity of land for cemeteries.

The third method is burial. The body may be buried below the ground in individual graves or above the ground in huge burial houses known as mausoleums. The shortage of land in many areas will demand more extensive use of mausoleums in the future.

Many people today are asking, Are funerals necessary? and Should we have a memorial service? Such services may not be necessary, but circumstances must always control the ceremony or lack of it. I have seen occasions when no burial service was held and the family of the deceased later regretted it.

One of the things that ought to be decided with due deliberation by any family is where the service should be held. My own feeling is—though ministers do not all agree at this point—that a church member's funeral ought to be held at the church. This would be in keeping with his life of faithfulness and devotion to the church.

I recognize that there are some good arguments against funeral services at the church. One is that our auditoriums are often large and not very suitable. The working man may find it difficult to get off work for a friend's funeral, so many of our friends have very few people in attendance. There is also an expense to the church when the funeral is held in the church auditorium. But when a person has put his life into the church, I feel that the church should open its doors to that individual, lovingly and willingly, and also to anyone else who would choose to use the church.

Always, I ask the family of the deceased if they want to have the funeral at the church for another reason. I have known some people to drop out of church following a funeral with the excuse that "I can't go back to church because the funeral was held there." The pastor's proper approach might be something like this: "We want you to have the service at the church if you wish, but bear in mind that it is going to be difficult, the first time, and other times, too."

How much should be spent? is another question that has to be raised. I have never felt it my responsibility to help a family make such a financial decision any more than I would select their automobile.

Often the expense of a funeral is something we are not prepared to accept because we have no idea what a reasonable cost is, and we avoid thinking about it. Every item we buy today seems excessively high—higher than last year, when it was higher than the year before. As pastors, we need to lead our people in advance to give some thought and attention to the financial arrangements for a funeral. This can become a problem, sometimes even a matter of contention, in a family.

The burial ought to be in keeping with the manner of life of the deceased. One church member shared with me how a funeral director advised him wisely that his father was a simple man; therefore, the funeral service should be simply and wisely planned as a tribute to him.

I believe the funeral service has some very definite therapeutic and theological values. One of the major objectives of the funeral service is to lead the relatives and loved ones to accept the death. This is most difficult. At no time in a person's life are his remains more obvious than at his funeral service. If identity is not respected in death, the dignity of life is impaired.

A survivor is in great danger of morbid, excessive grief if he refuses to accept the fact that the deceased is dead. It is my conviction that the presence of the body helps to heal the hurt and to further the acceptance of death. In some funerals I have conducted, the caskets were sealed or there was nothing more than a picture of the deceased on a table. This sometimes is necessary, but I think it intensifies the grief of the relatives.

As a pastor, I am often asked, "Should children go to a funeral service?" It seems to me that children also have to accept the fact that family members die. To hide this from the children may create real problems for them later.

Even though children may go to the funeral service, I always advise against taking very young children to the cemetery. It is difficult to explain to a child what burial in the earth has to do with a person who has gone to heaven.

Often a parent has little time for a child during the anguish of death and bereavement. Because of a parent's own grief, children may have to be left with strangers in strange places, where their fright and sense of loss is greatly increased. Later, when the children ask questions, the adults will be better able to cope with explanations.

Music is important during funerals. It should reflect the faith of the deceased or the faith of the family. I prefer to have congregational singing of the great songs of the Christian faith in funeral services for Christians.

Another change I would make in a memorial service is to leave off the obituary. After all, the family and friends know who the deceased is, and the information is available in the newspaper. There is no way a pastor can make an obituary comforting or even helpful. Yet I realize that with some people this would be breaking with tradition, and I respect the formality unless I have permission to do otherwise.

I have an objection, also, to the casket's remaining open during the entire service. Whether the family has it opened afterward for themselves or for others, the choice is totally up to them. But I feel that a closed casket during the service keeps the family from being so strongly drawn to what it contains. Thus, they are in a little better frame of mind to hear what the minister might say concerning the things of God.

There are also many theological values and truths that can be portrayed through a funeral service. The roots of many of our American funeral customs go back through Western civilization to early Judeo-Christian beliefs concerning the nature of God, man, and the hereafter. Some people insist that all funerals are unchristian, pagan, and barbaric. They have the right to evaluate services they have attended, but I don't feel this is true of all services.

God made man in dignity, and I believe his departure from the world should be in dignity. In the ancient world, it was a custom in some areas to stop a clock when someone died. The clock may be stopped, but whether we wish it or not, we must go on.

The survivors must survive; the living must go on living. They may not have any desire to live, but they really have no choice. How can we help them?

A funeral service ought to contain, if possible, a good word about the deceased. As a minister, however, I am not going to lie. There are times when it is simply better to say nothing. We must always find a gracious word for the bereaved, because they need comfort.

Above all other things, I think there ought to be a glorious word said about God.

There are really only a few things people want to hear about at a funeral service: heaven, the resurrection, the comfort of God. A lot of subjects are not suitable for a funeral service. We are really tied to our eternal hope, and this is the reassurance that the family and friends want.

Since death is real, grief is real; and there is a pattern in the grief process. No minister, musician, friend, or mortician should whip people into hysteria. At the same time, neither should anyone at the funeral be embarrassed into repression of grief. Many times I have asked families to leave one of the survivors alone for a moment. Just an extra thirty seconds may mean all the difference in the world, for there is not another moment of farewell like it.

To coerce by custom or to make people react as we think they ought is wrong. This is taking their individuality away from them. Let people be themselves. Let them react their own way, while remaining close at hand to help and to guide.

In a funeral service at the church, I try to move the family back at least two rows of pews. I think those last few minutes of reflection for the family should be undisturbed. I know I would like to think my own thoughts at such a time. I have seen people get in the habit of going down the aisle shaking hands with all the relatives. I choose to place the family where they will be spared some of this.

If one wishes to shake hands with the family and assure them of love and prayers, there is usually a long waiting period from the time the family is escorted from the building to the car and their departure in the funeral procession. This would be a far better time for friends to speak to them.

At the cemetery, the committal of the body ought to be as simple as possible. The committal is for family and friends, not for impression or counting cars. The words spoken there ought always to focus away from the silent city with its grief to the celestial city of God.

At this time, I pray for the friends who have helped, for those who have sent flowers and prepared food, for the doctors and nurses, and for those who have prepared the body for burial. It is a time when people need to realize how others around them care. This awareness is very necessary in the healing process of their grief.

In the New Testament we read how Jesus commended Mary for anointing him for his burial ahead of time. Her thoughtfulness, he said, would be remembered always.

Most bereaved hearts remember in some way—though it is not done for that reason—the thoughtfulness of everyone who helped and cared. Sometimes the only thing that can draw a bereaved person back to reality is the fact that people care.

I cannot agree with some current thinking that we should do away with the funeral service. If we do, we would be doing away not only with the dignity of the individual but also with something that helps people have a normal grief release. When the normal grief release is denied, delayed reaction problems may arise to cause unhappiness and despair.

The funeral service has therapeutic value as well as theological value. Jesus went to the grave of Lazarus as a friend. He still comes as a friend, but more than that, as Savior, God, and Comforter. And as friends we should always remind one another of his comforting words, "Lo, I am with you alway" (Matt. 28:20).

Part III

The Mourners and Grief

5.
She Is Not Dead
Carl E. Bates

(The death of a child)

And he cometh to the house of the ruler of the synagogue, and seeth the tumult, and them that wept and wailed greatly. And when he was come in, he saith unto them, Why make ye this ado, and weep? The [child] is not dead, but sleepeth.

And they laughed him to scorn. But when he had put them all out, he taketh the father and mother of the [child], and those who were with him, and entereth in where the [child] was lying.

And he took the [child] by the hand, and said unto her, Talitha cumi; which is, being interpreted, [Little girl], I say unto thee, arise.

And straightway the [child] arose, and walked; for she was of the age of twelve years. And they were astonished with a great astonishment. And he charged them straitly that no man should know it; and commanded that something should be given her to eat (Mark 5:38-43).

Sacred memories cluster around the death and burial of a child.

When a child is born, joys stir the hearts of parents which only they can know. Dreams for the future gather and flood their minds. Family schedules are rearranged in loving concern for this new addition.

If ill-mannered death should claim the child, their hearts feel a loss such as they have not sustained before. In this loss, affections are shocked in a way that no other loss brings. Grief is deep and tears flow unchecked. This has been the experience of families in all ages. It was so during our Lord's earthly ministry. Customs may change, but death and sorrow are common to all throughout the

SHE IS NOT DEAD

earth.

The inspired writer of the Gospel of Mark described the experience of one family who received what Jesus has to give the sorrowing.

Our Lord came to the house of a highly-placed religious leader. He could hear a great din. People were sobbing and weeping. Some of these had been hired to weep and wail. (Well, what does one do when he has cried until he cannot cry any more?)

Jesus, however, dealt with the situation. He entered the house and told both the family and the professional mourners that their demonstration was entirely out of place, "For," said he, "she is not dead, but sleepeth."

This statement holds the key to our Lord's comfort in the hour of death. What did he mean? Why did he say it?

First, he could have meant, "She is not dead because you *resemble* her."

The most sacred relationship in the earth is that of family. When a man and a woman stand before God to be joined in marriage, something new comes into existence which has never happened in all of history. Two lives are joined; genetic characteristics are united. In children born to that union, family resemblance is unmistakable.

It is true! She is not dead because of resemblance that will live until time shall be no more. Children, your mother is not dead; you bear her likeness. If she was a godly mother, your challenge is to resemble her in her likeness to our Lord.

Again, why did Jesus say, "She is not dead"?

He could have meant: "She is not dead because you *remember* her."

It has been estimated that the human brain with its ten billion electronic cells is capable of recalling sixteen trillion things. Our Lord indicated that memory will last beyond death. The story of Dives and Lazarus reminds us that this is true, so we could assume that this was in our Lord's statement.

In the hill country of my beloved adopted state of North Carolina, one is almost sure to hear them sing a song at their funerals entitled, "Precious Memories." I do not fault them for this. If one does not have somewhere in his life some precious memories, he is an object of pity. Some of life's deepest and richest experiences (as well as the saddest) are kept alive through memory. So, our Lord spoke truth when he said, "She is not dead"—because you remember, she is not dead.

But is that really what he meant? I think not.

I believe the truth of the statement is best understood if we hear him say, "She is not dead because of the *resurrection*."

Physical death is but the moving of the soul and spirit out of the physical body. For a while, these are separated by this experience men call death. However, there is a deeper death than this, that is, separation from God forever, which is known as spiritual death. Our Lord is victorious over both.

He is the resurrection and the life. He restores both a renewed and a never-ending life. The touch of his hand is all that is needed.

For this reason we can say with James Whitcomb Riley:

> I cannot say, and I will not say
> That he is dead. He is just away.
>
> With a cheery smile, and a wave of the hand,
> He has wandered into an unknown land.
>
> And left us dreaming how very fair
> It needs must be, since he lingers there.
>
> And you—O you, who the wildest yearn
> For the old-time step and the glad return—
>
> Think of him faring on, as dear
> In the love of there as the love of here;
>
> Think of him still as the same, I say;
> He is not dead—he is just away!

6.
The Language of Sorrow
Charles G. Fuller

*(A funeral message on the occasion of the
death of one unknown to the minister.)*

The language of sorrow has a vocabulary all its own. Even by those who might attempt to master it, this language is not as well understood as by those who have been compelled to live for a time in the land of sorrow. There, words like *loneliness* are understood in the depths of the heart, as are words like *comfort, reassurance,* and *peace.*

Feeble indeed are attempts to interpret the language of sorrow by those who have not learned it through experience. But blessed indeed are fitly chosen words like, "I know how you feel," when they are spoken by one who *does* know the feel of bereavement.

Because some of you can speak from experience, you have something timely and helpful to offer these family members with whom we meet in remembrance of their loved one. Also, because our Lord Jesus Christ tasted of life as we experience it and submitted himself to death as we know it, he has something vital to say to us.

When Christ speaks of death and victory over it, his words are tempered with understanding and authenticity.

Just listen to the Lord speak through his Word: "I am the resurrection, and the life: he that believeth in me, though he were dead, yet shall he live: and whosoever liveth and believeth in me shall never die" (John 11:25–26).

Also, the beautiful and well-loved passage:

> *Let not your heart be troubled: ye believe in God, believe also in me. In my Father's house are many mansions: if it were not so, I would have told you.*
>
> *I go to prepare a place for you. And if I go and prepare a place for you, I will come again, and receive you unto myself; that where I am, there ye may be also. And whither I go ye know, and the way ye know.*
>
> *Thomas saith unto him, Lord, we know not whither thou goest; and how can we know the way?*
>
> *Jesus saith unto him, I am the way, the truth, and the life: no man cometh unto the Father, but by me (John 14:1–6).*

Death and sorrow do have a language of their own. And it is true that such a language is best understood among those who have been left behind by the loss of a loved one. But there are some things which death and sorrow may say to anyone who will listen.

Even this friend and loved one, whose memory we are met to recall, speaks to us from the experience of death. We listened to him as he spoke in life, surely we will listen as his experience of death speaks to each of us.

First, his death has something very pointed to say about

The Nature of Life

Life, at its best, is unpredictable. We cannot measure its days in advance. We grow accustomed to having our loved ones around us. It will not always be that way, we realize, but somehow we cannot quite imagine what life would be like without our family members dotted about the earth and around our lives.

Then suddenly, we are confronted with the bleak fact that one dear to us is gone. It is then that we realize how tenderly accurate the Scriptures are when they tell us:

> *Go to now, ye that say, To day or to morrow we will go into such a city, and continue there a year, and buy and sell, and get gain:*

> *Whereas ye know not what shall be on the morrow. For what is your life? It is even a vapor, that appeareth for a little time, and then vanisheth away. For that ye ought to say, If the Lord will, we shall live, and do this, or that (Jas. 4:13–15).*

Through his death, our friend whose memory we recall today reminds us that none of us are exempt or immune from life with its joys, its sorrows, or its unpredictable conclusion.

That is why our heavenly Father has spoken out of his earnest desire to help us understand and deal with the truth and has inspired candid lines of Scripture such as, "It is appointed unto men once to die, but after this the judgment" (Heb. 9:27).

Today our friend speaks through his death, telling those of us who meet about his memory that life is of such nature that we must not take it for granted.

Then, too, his death has something very vital to say about

The Need of a Savior

God himself, knowing our need for someone to deal with death when it comes to us, took loving initiative and sent his only Son to defeat the results of death. That is why Christ came to earth—to assume, in our behalf, the guilt of our sin and to deliver us from the defeat death would otherwise claim over us.

That is why we need a Savior. With Christ as Savior, we can have victory over death and the grave.

Years ago, Paul wrote about the victory we have through Christ over the grave:

> *So when this corruptible shall have put on incorruption, and this mortal shall have put on immortality, then shall be brought to pass the saying that is written, Death is swallowed up in victory. O death, where is thy sting? O grave, where is thy victory? The sting of death is sin; and the strength of sin is the law. But thanks be to God, which giveth us the victory through our Lord Jesus Christ (1 Cor. 15:54–57).*

Surely, when we comprehend the nature of life, we readily see our need for a Savior and we wisely entrust our lives to Christ. It is as the psalmist wrote in the long ago, "So teach us to number our days, that we may apply our hearts unto wisdom" (90:12).

The whole perspective on death and sorrow is changed when we have Christ as our Savior. Perhaps the apostle Paul best reflects that perspective in his succinct statement not long before he passed into eternity, "For to me to live is Christ, and to die is gain" (Phil. 1:21).

There is still another reminder which comes to us in the midst of our friend's death and that has to do with

The Nearness of God

If we could hear our loved ones from the other side of eternity speaking to us just now, surely they would encourage us to claim the nearness of God, for he is close at hand. The psalmist said, "Thou art near, O Lord; and all thy commandments are truth" (119:151).

And he also wrote:

> *The Lord is my light and my salvation; whom shall I fear? the Lord is the strength of my life; of whom shall I be afraid? . . . For in the time of trouble he shall hide me in his pavilion: in the secret of his tabernacle shall he hide me; he shall set me up upon a rock . . . . Wait on the Lord: be of good courage, and he shall strengthen thine heart: wait, I say, on the Lord (27:1,5,14).*

God is near. He is near to comfort and strengthen you whose hearts are heavy in the loss of your loved one. For, indeed, "God is our refuge and strength, a very present help in trouble" (Ps. 46:1).

God is near. He is near in the person of the Holy Spirit to minister through his understanding of life and its trials. Remember as God, the Son, he experienced life in the flesh as we know it.

THE LANGUAGE OF SORROW 57

> *For we have not an high priest which cannot be touched with the feeling of our infirmities; but was in all points tempted like as we are, yet without sin. Let us therefore come boldly unto the throne of grace, that we may obtain mercy, and find grace to help in time of need (Heb. 4:15–16).*

God is near. He wants to take the language of this experience called death and sorrow and translate it into the assurance of the prophet of old: "The Lord is good, a strong hold in the day of trouble; and he knoweth them that trust in him" (Nah. 1:7).

7.
Not Dead, Just Moved Away
Herschel H. Hobbs

For we know that if our earthly house of this tabernacle were dissolved, we have a building of God, an house not made with hands, eternal in the heavens (2 Cor. 5:1).

We have come together for these brief moments to do honor to the memory of one we loved and have lost for a little while. It is not necessary to spend these moments in eulogy, for you knew him. Each of you has a precious possession hidden in your treasure house of memory. We would not profane that memory by invading its privacy. Rather, we would leave it as your own personal gem to be enjoyed in the secrecy of your own heart.

Suffice to say that he was a Christian. And that is all that really matters in this hour. At this moment the important thing is not how much wealth one accumulates, or how much fame adheres to one's name. The vital thing is what he did with Jesus, who is called Christ. Brother A. trusted Christ in his life; he has found him trustworthy in death.

So that we do not sorrow as those without hope. Tears may flow from our eyes, but assurance is in our hearts. And through these tears God's love shines, making a rainbow of promise upon our souls. We sorrow. Yes! But it is for ourselves. Our dear one has preceded us to be with the Lord, leaving us behind. And we are lonely. He has slipped through the veil to dwell eternally in the Father's house of many mansions prepared by the Savior for his own. Thus while we sorrow for ourselves, we rejoice for him.

This is what Paul is saying in 2 Corinthians 5:1: "For we know that if our earthly house of this tabernacle were dissolved, we have a building of God, an house not made with hands, eternal in the heavens."

The word *know* means perceptive knowledge or a conviction of the soul. Thus with the apostle and with all believers it is not "maybe," "perhaps," or simply "hope." It is assurance born out of a conviction which God by our faith has planted in our souls.

"Tabernacle" means "tent," which suggests a temporary dwelling. It is the dwelling place of nomads. In the evening it is set up, held in place only by pegs driven into the sand. The next morning it is struck down, folded up, and its occupant moves on to another tent site for the coming evening. Indeed, the words *were dissolved* translate a verb which means to strike down a tent.

Paul, therefore, saw the human body as a tent. When John 1:14 speaks of Jesus Christ becoming flesh to dwell among us, the word for "dwelt" means to live in a tent. He lived temporarily among us in a tent of flesh. This is what our loved one has done.

It is said that in the human body there is a constant process of old cells dying and new ones being formed. So that every seven years we have an entirely new body. This dear man, therefore, has lived in several bodies. We did not weep for him when he moved from the first to the second or the fifth to the sixth. Why then should we weep when he moved from the body before us into the house of many mansions?

No, for him we rejoice as we weep for ourselves. He is like Abraham, of whom Hebrews 11:9—10 says that he lived in Canaan in tents, but "he looked for a city which hath foundations, whose builder and maker is God" (v. 10). And he has found that city.

This is what Paul was saying. When this old earthly tent is worn out and is no longer fit for habitation, we move from it into "a building of God, an house not made with hands, eternal in the heavens." A building has a foundation, suggesting permanent dwelling. It is our dwelling place prepared by God, and it is eternal in the heavens.

Let us suppose that for these many years your loved one had lived in a once lovely neighborhood in a nice home. But through the years the community has run down and the house was ready to fall down. Then one day he learned that he had fallen heir to a beautiful mansion in the most elite section of the city. You would rejoice with him as he moved into his new home. Your only sadness would be that you were left alone in the old neighborhood.

Well, that is what has happened to him now. He is in that place of many mansions, living in "a building of God, an house not made with hands, eternal in the heavens."

Paul's words assure us that, at what we call death, the soul does not exist in an unconscious state until the final resurrection. We cannot see a man of Paul's nature looking forward to such a condition. In 2 Corinthians 5:6,8 he said, "Therefore we are always confident, knowing that, whilst we are at home in the body, we are absent from the Lord . . . . We are confident, I say, and willing rather to be absent from the body, and to be present with the Lord." Note the words "absent from the body . . . present with the Lord." No in between.

Thus your believing loved one is now with the Lord. He is more alive, aware, and conscious now than he has ever been before.

A doctor once told me that death is as much a part of life as is birth. Now in that light, just suppose that in his prenatal state Brother A. could have reasoned. He would have said, "Something is about to happen to me. I am fixing to leave the only place of life I have ever known. This must be death." When in reality he found that it was not death, but birth: birth out of the narrow confines of his mother's womb into a far broader, greater, and richer life.

In the same vein, let us suppose, a few hours ago another

change was about to take place. And again he reasoned, "Something is about to happen to me. I am about to leave the only place of life I have ever known. Surely this must be death."

But if he could now speak to us in audible tones, he would say, "No, I was wrong again. What I thought was death was another birth. A birth out of the comparative life I had known in my fleshly body into the superlative life of heaven—richer and grander than my fondest dreams, faith, and hope ever imagined."

What we dimly view from afar by faith he now knows clearly by experience and sight. He is with the Lord. The Lord is with us. And in the Lord we are together forevermore!

8.
Victory in Jesus
Landrum Leavell

(On the death of an eighteen-month-old child)

This occasion confronts us with life's greatest enigma, death. It is referred to in the Word of God as "the last enemy." Though the busy mind of modern man has probed the heights of the heavens and plumbed the depths of the seas, he can offer no satisfactory solution to this universal experience.

An old song, widely sung by our forefathers, both asks and answers a question. The question is, "Does Jesus care?" The ringing affirmation of the chorus brings us comfort at this time: "Oh, yes, he cares, I know he cares!"

Proof of that is found in the blessed book in Matthew 19:13–15. There we read, "Then were there brought unto him little children, that he should put his hands on them, and pray; and the disciples rebuked them. But Jesus said, Suffer little children, and forbid them not, to come unto me; for of such is the kingdom of heaven. And he laid his hands on them, and departed thence." If you have ever wondered if Jesus cares for little children, the answer is found once and for all in this passage.

Today we are faced with

Perplexity

Our perplexity is expressed in the question mark. It is our tendency to ask why, especially in light of problems which we cannot readily solve. Even as we search for solutions, we know all the while there is no ready answer to the untimely death of a little child.

There are some things which we do know with assurance. We know that "it is appointed unto men once to die, but after that the judgment" (Heb. 9:27). We do know that death is both universal and impartial, for death takes no holiday and is no respecter of persons.

For all of us as parents, who feel a particular empathy at a time like this, we quickly face the fact that God does not give us children with a guarantee of longevity. We are not granted the privilege of parenthood with any immunity to heartache. We vaguely comprehend the fact that if we provide our children with an automobile, there is a lurking possibility that the child may be involved in a fatal automobile accident. We teach our children to swim, for there exists the spectre of drowning. Even the most accomplished swimmer may find himself in difficulty and lose his life in the water.

Some of life's most perplexing questions center in the continuation of disease, war, famine, and pestilences of every kind. Our hearts cry out to know why God does not step in to put an end to such suffering.

I can provide no pat answers, but for the Christian these must all relate to doxology, not theology. In all things we are to give thanks. The Bible assures us that it is the Lord who gives and the Lord who takes away, as Job said. In the midst of our question marks, we can unite trembling voices in exclaiming, "Blessed be the name of the Lord!"

In the Christian scheme of things, every human life has

Purpose

We ask ourselves, what was Joey's purpose? Perhaps the answer will continue to unfold throughout the lives of parents and friends, but again we have certain assurances.

Joey stretched the capacity of his parents to love. His parents loved him devotedly and cared for him sacrificially. Experiences such as those through which they have come will leave an indelible impression in their lives and ministry.

This young life, though brief, experienced the wonderful joy of being wanted and adored. No Christian can fail to reach out to another human in need, but few things are as moving as the helplessness of a child during critical illness. Even as Joey received love, he gave love. He had little else to offer, but what a rich and unforgettable gift to receive love from such a one!

The brief life of this little fellow increased our capacity to respond in compassion to others. Any parent on earth who has lost a son can have understanding and love for these dear friends today.

Sometime ago, a vacationing preacher friend visited a northern orchard. It was at the time of the harvest of apples, and he saw the burdened apple trees propped up to keep the limbs from breaking under the weight of the fruit. With great interest, he questioned the owner of the orchard. How did this sort of thing happen? What was the secret of such a bountiful harvest? The owner responded that he also found it somewhat a mystery, but would share something that had happened many years before.

He led the preacher to the base of a tree, where a large, ugly scar was obvious to the eye. The scar had healed over with the bark of the trunk. The preacher confessed that he could see the tree had been damaged and asked what had happened. The owner answered that in the beginning, when the trees were young, too much of the tree was going into wood, and not enough into fruit. It was discovered that if the tree was scarred, more of its strength would go into fruit and less into trunk and branches.

Christians understand that we are in the fruit business. Hebrews (12:6) reminds us that "whom the Lord loveth he chasteneth." We are also told, "But if ye be without chastisement, whereof all are partakers, then are ye illegitimate, and not sons" (12:8). God does not deal with us as with criminals being punished for wrongdoing. But he deals with us as children who are disciplined for the good which they may accomplish.

Now, we need to remember God's

Provision

Our blessed Lord promised, "I will not leave you comfortless." That means he provides for us when the need is present. Perhaps one day these sorrowing parents will look back on this experience with the knowledge that Jesus Christ was never more real to them than in this hour of need.

Jesus also provided for our need when he asserted, "I am the resurrection, and the life: he that believeth in me, though he were dead, yet shall he live. And whosoever liveth and believeth in me shall never die" (John 11:25). This precious promise, echoing down through the corridors of time, speaks peace to our troubled hearts.

Heaven is Christ's provision for all his children. According to the book of Revelation, "God shall wipe away all tears from their eyes" (21:4). This affirms that there will be no tears in heaven, but glorious and joyous reunion with our Lord and his people forevermore. Because of our anticipation of that indescribable event, we find our hearts singing, "Oh, victory in Jesus, my Savior, forever!"

9.
The Blessed Dead
Jaroy Weber

> *And I heard a voice from heaven saying unto me, Write, Blessed are the dead which die in the Lord from henceforth: Yea, saith the Spirit, that they may rest from their labours; and their works do follow them (Rev. 14:13).*

Death is an experience in silence. Suddenly there seems nothing that the preacher, poet, or philosopher can say, but surely God has a word.

One of God's most comforting words to us about death is, "Blessed are those who die in the Lord." The word *blessed* literally means "happy." The child of God is happy because he is with him. I know Mrs. H. is happy because I'm sure God is fulfilling her desire to play the piano for a thousand years and sing for a thousand years.

When we come to a time like this, the question, Why? always confronts us.

Yet there is no human answer to suffering. Many of the reasons people try to give are not valid. Certainly we do not suffer because God *wants* to break our hearts, for Jesus was grieved at suffering. Neither does God *want* to add misery to this world, for Jesus wept over the suffering of cities.

At this moment of question, there are some things I do know. We are God's children and he loves us! Nothing in this world can separate us from the love of God. Cancer can touch the body, but not the soul.

We have no reason to be *ignorant*.

We can be confident of the providence of God. "All things work together for good to them that love God . . ." (Rom. 8:28). We don't always understand this, but we know it is true. Mrs. H. accomplished more for God in her suffering than most people do in their health. She gave evidence of the adequacy of God's grace to a believer.

We are reminded of the presence of evil. We live in a world which is evil and as human beings we share in the human experiences of good and bad, happiness and tragedy, joy and pain.

Yet we can always rely on the provision of God's grace. He gives to us saving grace, keeping grace, and when we come to the end of life, he also gives dying grace. Mrs. H. loved God and believed this. It was a truth she counted on for courage.

We have no need to be *comfortless*.

Now she is enjoying "rest from [her] labours."

There comes a time when God will take each of us out of this world of grief and sorrow. For these long months she labored in suffering faithfully, enduring it with courage for the sake of family and friends. But now she is at rest with God. This work of faith brings peace which passeth all understanding. Only the true Christian understands this contentment.

We can take comfort because we know the meaning and also the Master of death. It is a sleep, a departure from this body to be with the Lord. It is a homegoing, where God has prepared for us a place not made with hands. It is not defeat, it is triumph!

We have no cause to be *defeated*.

"Their works do follow them," we are told. And we are sure that her works do follow her where she has gone.

This puts the works of our lives in proper perspective. They are not sent up to heaven to save us, but they follow after as a testimony of our salvation. What she has done for God, church, and family, she did in love, even through suffering. What she did will testify to God on her behalf.

A mystic has said: "Death is not the extinguishing of the light. It is the putting out of the candle because the dawn has come."

And also, about Mrs. H. it can be said, even as it was by Peter Marshall concerning mothers: "Nothing that has ever been said, that could be said, or ever will be said, would be eloquent enough or adequate to make articulate that peculiar emotion we feel for our mothers."

10.
The Good Man
Russell H. Dilday, Jr.

Psalm 1

One of the many questions we find ourselves asking in the presence of death is: How does one evaluate the worth of life? In this solemn moment, it is obvious that the traditional measurements of success don't apply at all. How much wealth a man accumulated, how big a business he built, how widely known his reputation, what clubs and organizations he belonged to—obviously, these questions cannot give an ultimate measure of the worth of a life.

We discover, instead, that the biblical concept of a man is really the only basis upon which to measure a life. Psalm 1 describes those qualities which make life truly great, truly prosperous, genuinely successful and complete. The psalmist must have had someone like Mr. L. in mind when he gave us this description of a good man.

A Good Man Is Morally Stabilized

"Blessed is the man that walketh not in the counsel of the ungodly, nor standeth in the way of sinners, nor sitteth in the seat of the scornful" (v. 1).

A good man recognizes the pernicious danger of evil. He is aware that sin, once allowed into one's life, inevitably intensifies and grows until a man who is willing to walk with the ungodly will soon be willing to stand in the way of sinners and ultimately will be willing and comfortable to sit in the seat of the scornful.

This man had the kind of moral stability that kept him from that danger. He had an alert dedication to what was right. He could see through the subtle deception of wrong and he put down his moral stakes, refusing to drop his guard or let sin get a foothold on the territory of his life. He walked not "in the counsel of the ungodly, nor [stood] in the way of sinners, nor [sat] in the seat of the scornful." His life was morally stabilized.

A Good Man Is Spiritually Oriented

"But his delight is in the law of the Lord; and in his law doth he meditate day and night" (v. 2).

Like the man described in this psalm, Mr. L. was spiritually programmed. His primary interest and ultimate goals were spiritual. His whole life was centered around his faith in Jesus Christ.

We have all known him to be a man who loved the Lord, loved the church, loved the Bible. And this verse says that is what ultimately identifies a full and meaningful life: one whose delight is in the law of the Lord, one who meditates upon it day and night, one who is spiritually oriented.

A Good Man Is Deeply Rooted

"And he shall be like a tree planted by the rivers of water, that bringeth forth his fruit in his season; his leaf also shall not wither; and whatsoever he doeth shall prosper" (v. 3).

His life was like that—rooted in rich soil of prayer, worship, Bible study. He drew his strength from his personal relationship with Christ, through which the life of any man becomes deeply rooted, "like a tree planted by the rivers of water."

A Good Man Is Creatively Productive

"He bringeth forth his fruit . . ." (v. 3).

Most of the human accomplishment we are so proud of in life

becomes insignificant and anemic in the presence of death. But this passage in verse 3 reminds us that the work we do for the Lord in his kingdom, through his church, is lasting and valuable.

Mr. L. bore that kind of fruit in faithful service through the church, in leading others to faith in Christ, in cultivating the Christlike spirit. His wife reminded me that he enjoyed reading Psalm 92:12–14.

A Good Man Is Eternally Secure

"For the Lord knoweth the way of the righteous: but the way of the ungodly shall perish" (v. 6).

Here is a beautiful promise: the man who rejects sin, centers his life in faith in Jesus Christ, sinks his roots deeply into the power of the Spirit and bears the fruit of Christian service, shall not perish, but have everlasting life.

Mr. L. had no doubt about his eternal security. He quoted Paul often: "I know whom I have believed, and am persuaded that he is able to keep that which I have committed unto him against that day" (2 Tim. 1:12).

Today we are grateful for this simple but profound description of the good man. And we are grateful for the example of our friend, who with God's help exemplified that happy and abundant life. It reminds us that we, too, should be morally stabilized, spiritually oriented, deeply rooted, creatively productive, and eternally secure.

11.
On Healing Troubled Hearts
James L. Pleitz

Jesus Christ, the great physician, was—and is—the great heart specialist. Although he is quite capable of handling any problem, his specialty is troubled hearts.

Over two thousand years ago, he spoke some beautiful and comforting words to his disciples. As believers, we can claim them as our very own.

> *Let not your heart be troubled: ye believe in God, believe also in me. In my Father's house are many mansions: if it were not so, I would have told you. I go to prepare a place for you. And if I go and prepare a place for you, I will come again, and receive you unto myself; that where I am, there ye may be also (John 14:1–3).*

These words of our Master speak to our hearts today in a strange and wonderful way. Our hearts, too, are troubled. When our loved ones are taken by death, we too are shaken.

As Christians, we should not hesitate to give expression to our grief. We should never bottle up our tears. There is nothing contradictory about seeing a saint of God with a tear-stained face. Paul said, "We sorrow not, even as others which have no hope" (1 Thess. 4:13). The sorrow of the Christian is different from the sorrow of one who does not believe. But when death comes, we still know the pangs of sorrow. At the grave of Lazarus, Jesus himself wept.

Christ said that the cure for troubled hearts is belief: belief in God and belief in him. "Ye believe in God, believe also in me."

What we believe about God and our Savior brings peace to our troubled hearts today.

We believe that our heavenly Father cares when our hearts are troubled. The Bible pictures God in many ways. First, he is pictured as the great Creator. He is also pictured as Judge and as King. Jesus most frequently pictured God as Father. He is the perfect, loving, heavenly Father.

When Jesus taught his disciples to pray, "Our Father, which art in heaven," he was not primarily concerned with teaching them where the Father was. His concern was with teaching them what kind of Father God is. He is the perfect Father. A Father like this cares when his children have troubled hearts.

Up until then, this conversation of Jesus with his disciples had been about life and death issues. "And fear not them which kill the body, but are not able to kill the soul: but rather fear him which is able to destroy both soul and body in hell" (Matt. 10:28).

Jesus scarcely paused before he went on to say, "Are not two sparrows sold for a farthing? and one of them shall not fall on the ground without your Father. But the very hairs of your head are all numbered. Fear ye not therefore, ye are of more value than many sparrows" (Matt. 10:29–31). It seems a strange time for Jesus to talk about birds. But the heavenly Father who is concerned about sparrows certainly is concerned about us.

The picture Jesus paints is not necessarily of a sparrow falling from the sky in a death spiral. Perhaps he was describing a little sparrow who trips and falls on the ground as he hops about looking for food. How infinitely great is the concern of our heavenly Father. The fact that he knows the numbers of hairs on our heads not only speaks of his infinite knowledge, but his infinite love. We can trust a God like that to heal our broken hearts.

A young man who had surrendered to the ministry became very discouraged while studying in the seminary. He wrote his pastor back in his home church and told him about his problems. The wise pastor answered the young man's letter by sending him this poem:

> Said the robin to the wren, "I would surely like to know
> Why these restless human beings rush about and worry so."
> Said the wren to the robin, "I think surely it must be
> That they have no Heavenly Father such as cares for you and me."

That poem completely changed the direction of the boy's life. The knowledge that someone does care works wonders to cure broken hearts. We do have a heavenly Father and he does care.

When our hearts are troubled, we can rest assured that God cares. There is no power on the face of the earth that can separate us from his love.

> *Who shall separate us from the love of Christ? shall tribulation, or distress, or persecution, or famine, or nakedness, or peril, or sword? As it is written, For thy sake we are killed all the day long; we are accounted as sheep for the slaughter. Nay, in all these things we are more than conquerors through him that loved us. For I am persuaded, that neither death, nor life, nor angels, nor principalities, nor powers, nor things present, nor things to come, nor height, nor depth, nor any other creature, shall be able to separate us from the love of God, which is in Christ Jesus our Lord (Rom. 8:35-39).*

God heals our troubled hearts by assuring us that he has prepared a place for us in the Father's house.

The Bible gives us a number of glimpses of our heavenly home. John said in Revelation 21:19,21: "The foundations of the walls of the city were garnished with all manner of precious stones . . . . And the twelve gates were twelve pearls: every gate was of one pearl: and the street of the city was pure gold, as it were transparent glass."

Jesus himself said, quite simply, "Heaven is like the Father's house."

It has been years since I lived in my father's house, but I still have many fond memories of that wonderful place. We had a lot of fun at my father's house. We played with rubber guns and old car tires. (I spent many a day pushing a tire up and down the street.) We built bag swings and skate skooters. We played "chalk the corner" and hide-and-seek and "kick the can." There was no expense involved in any one of these games. We had a wonderful time in our father's house.

More importantly, our father's house was a place of love and warmth and understanding. This is not to say that I always understood the actions of my father, but I never questioned his love. In time, the understanding would come.

Many times it's hard for us to understand the actions of our heavenly Father. Even Paul, who had such a perfect understanding of the heart and mind of God, said, "Now we see through a glass, darkly; but then face to face: now I know in part; but then shall I know even as also I am known" (1 Cor. 13:12).

The knowledge that our loved ones are with Jesus in the Father's house brings peace to our troubled hearts.

A little boy was telling a friend the story of Enoch. He said, "God and Enoch were very good friends. Every day they used to take long walks together. One day they walked a long, long way together. When Enoch turned to go home, God said, 'Enoch, we're closer to my house than yours. Why don't you just come and go home with me.' And he did."

The little fellow may have gotten some of his facts confused, but he was right about one thing. At death, the believer is assured of a home in the Father's house with Almighty God.

12.
Our Eternal Home
W. Randall Lolley

There are some things that a wise man simply does not do. A wise man will never read the book of Jonah as a whaling manual. A wise man will not read the Gettysburg Address just for its punctuation. A wise man will never stand in a room like this on a day like this and try to summarize with a lick and a promise and a rushed-up prayer the impact on all of us made by a public servant like J. G.

He stayed much too busy to hear our accolades while he was with us managing the business of our city. I have an idea he is much too busy now to hear our words of praise. Thank God, we are spared the pain of having to scratch and paw back along the path of this pilgrim for some just-right word to describe him.

Public Servant—that is our word. It says it all. For three score years and four he lived, in his adult life a public servant who every day gave just a little bit more of himself away to the people and to the city he loved—that was this man.

J. G. was a bird hunter, too. Quite a few stories circulate in the parts as to his prowess in that sport. Bird hunters get up early and stay up late. They see many a sunrise and many a sunset.

Strange, isn't it, how remarkably similar the colors are of a dawn and a sunset? We could easily confuse the two. But make no mistake about it, the colors that are gathered here now around the path of this good man are not the somber tones of evening but the brilliant hues of morning. He has not slipped into a darkening sunset where all the lights go out. He has entered into a glorious dawn where the lights come on. That was his hope, and it is our Christian hope, too. Thus we sorrow, but not as those who do not have our hope.

Perhaps one of the ancient Proverbs of Israel says it best: "The path of the just is as the shining light" (4:18).

J. G. was more than just a man, even just a prominent man, he was a just man. His church family loved him, and he loved his church. Here we sometimes sing a song, the words of which have somehow been ringing in my mind for the past forty-eight hours. It seems that the song says something that he would want said here.

> O God, our help in ages past,
> Our hope for years to come;
> Our shelter from the stormy blast
> And our eternal home.
>
> —Isaac Watts

So hear this public servant's song:

1. It speaks of ***God, a help in ages past.***

J. G. was one of the most unselfish men I have ever known. He did not have to be on camera or scream from the headlines to get things done. He loved people and he entrusted to them the destiny of this city. He discovered that it was easier to help than to be helped. Yet he agreed with Israel's ancient psalmist when he asked, "From whence cometh my help?" And also when he answered, "My help comes from the Lord, which made heaven and earth" (121:1–2).

No matter what the deeds in the county courthouse may say, J. G. believed this city belonged to the Lord. It was his long before it was anyone else's. So J. G. never presumed to ask God to do something for him that he could do for himself. And he did not take on tasks by himself which only God could do.

Then he discovered something important: God's work and his

work were strangely one and the same in this city.

The helped are made for helping. Our Creator has given us two hands. Maybe, just maybe, he meant us to have one to receive with and one to give with. If we fail to fulfill this rhythm, we become a stale cistern instead of a fresh channel in this world.

J. G. was helped in order that he might be a helper. His help came to him from the Lord on its way to someone else.

2. His song speaks of **God, a hope for years to come.**

J. G. possessed an unquenchable hope, or, to say it better, an unquenchable hope possessed him. He looked into the teeth of a culture's doubting darkness and dared to smile. He knew full well, during those twenty-one years at the helm, that the awesome urban problems which blighted the cities of America would not stop at the city limits of Winston-Salem. Yet his hope, his confidence in his God, his colleagues, and himself, gave him grit and gall to fight back.

A large part of the reason he dared stay young, think young, react young was his robust hope. His hope gave him a love for life. Hope skipped and danced its way through his life until he could join the early Christians in saying not, "Look what the world's coming to," but, "Look what's come to the world."

3. His song speaks of **God, a shelter from the stormy blast.**

Shelters can be either helpful or treacherous things. On the one hand, a shelter can become an escape hatch to keep one isolated and insulated from life out there in the weather where people hurt. On the other hand, a shelter can become a temporary rest stop where one gains resources to face the stormy blasts.

The living God was that latter kind of shelter for our friend. He was no whistle-blowing patrolman whose main concern was safety. He was an ordnance officer handing out tools.

J. G. worshiped because he knew how much work he had to do, and in that rhythm of worship and work, he found his peace.

4. His song speaks of **God, an eternal home.**

In J. G.'s vocabulary, there was no more pleasant word than "home." He was in the best sense a family man. His home and his happiness were one and the same.

Yet the thought of his belonging to the family of God kept him strong. That family now has claimed him. There is left to each of us a folder of unfinished business.

Perhaps our newspapers today said it best:

> Someone will succeed him as City Manager, but there is a strong feeling among those who worked with him and knew him best that he won't be replaced, that you just don't replace a man like J. G. . . . Suffice it to say that with luck the city of Winston-Salem will have good management in the future, but whatever successes we achieve in the years to come will be built on the remarkable record of a quiet and remarkable man.

13.
The Hope of Seeing Jesus
James W. Bryant

In the Bible there are three beautiful pictures of the victory and hope which the child of God, having committed his heart and life to Jesus, has through our Lord and Savior, Jesus Christ. There is the hope of seeing Jesus face to face at the moment of death. Even more, there is the hope of seeing Jesus face to face at the moment of his return. And there is the hope of our bodies being raised again one day, made incorruptible and brand new, forever to stand in the presence of the Lord to the praise of his glory.

The apostle Paul expected to see the returning Jesus face to face in his own lifetime. And yet Paul died without Jesus coming again. I have often wondered, when Paul knelt before the executioner on the Appian Way outside Rome, even while the sword made its downward swish through the air, if he did not think, *Jesus may come back before the sharp edge of that blade touches the back of my neck.* He expected to see Jesus face to face. And he taught the people to whom he wrote that same hope.

The Thessalonian Christians to whom Paul wrote so much about the victory of Christ's return held on to that hope with joyful anticipation. And yet their loved ones began to die before Jesus came back to bring with him the everlasting life he had promised. So they began to ask, What about these who have died; have they been cheated of our great hope in Christ? Will they be able to share in the glorious victory that we anticipate as Christians who are alive remaining until his coming?

Paul answered them with the following words:

THE HOPE OF SEEING JESUS

> *But I would not have you to be ignorant, brethren, concerning them which are asleep, that ye sorrow not, even as others which have no hope. For if we believe that Jesus died and rose again, even so them also which sleep in Jesus will God bring with him. For this we say unto you by the word of the Lord, that we which are alive and remain unto the coming of the Lord shall not prevent them which are asleep. For the Lord himself shall descend from heaven with a shout, with the voice of the archangel and the trump of God: and the dead in Christ shall rise first: Then we which are alive and remain shall be caught up together with them in the clouds, to meet the Lord in the air: and so shall we ever be with the Lord (1 Thess. 4:13-18).*

Paul added, "Wherefore comfort one another with these words," which is what we seek to do on every funeral day.

Paul said that the man in Christ who dies, just as much as he who continues to live until the day of Christ's return, will share in the same victory in Jesus. The dead in Christ and those still alive in that day when Jesus comes again will meet together in the clouds of the sky. "And," the Scriptures say, "so shall we ever be with the Lord." For those who know Christ, there is never a final good-bye; it is just "so long"; it is just "until we meet again"; it is just "until tomorrow."

That great Presbyterian preacher, Peter Marshall, said to his wife as they put him in the ambulance to take him to the hospital, where he died of a heart attack, "Catherine, I'll see you in the morning."

That is the Christian hope. All of us who know Jesus will share together in that victory. If we die, we go to be with Jesus. Our hope at the moment of death, and our hope in Jesus' return are not different in kind, only in timing. Paul assures all of us that, whether we live or die, we can expect to see Jesus face to face.

What Happens When We Die?

I wonder if perhaps the Christians in Thessalonica then began to ask: But what happens to us in the meantime? What happens to our loved ones when they die?

I suppose we wonder about that philosophically until death stalks into our home and snatches from us one dearer than life itself. Then it is no longer a philosophical question but a personal one. Where is he? Is he safe? Does he suffer any longer? Is he lonely? What about those who die in the Lord?

God, through the apostle Paul, put together another chapter in the Bible, a passage which strengthens the hope that we have of seeing Jesus face to face. Perhaps Paul himself was in the presence of death when he said,

> For we know that if our earthly house of this tabernacle were dissolved, we have a building of God, an house not made with hands, eternal in the heavens. For in this we groan, earnestly desiring to be clothed upon with our house which is from heaven: if so be that being clothed we shall not be found naked. For we that are in this tabernacle do groan, being burdened: not for that we would be unclothed, but clothed upon, that mortality might be swallowed up of life.
>
> Now he that hath wrought us for the selfsame thing is God, who also hath given unto us the earnest of the Spirit. Therefore, we are always confident, knowing that, whilst we are at home in the body, we are absent from the Lord (for we walk by faith, not by sight): we are confident, I say, and willing rather to be absent from the body, and to be present with the Lord (2 Cor. 5:1–8).

I am so glad God put that chapter in his book, because it enables me to say to a loving and grieving family that the moment a Christian closes his eyes in death on earth, he opens his eyes in life in heaven. To be absent from the body is to be present instantly with the Lord. We have that hope as Christians. Even though the body of a man dies, his spirit, the man himself, that which is inside, goes in a moment into the very presence of Jesus, in happiness and in glory to await the day when Jesus comes back to reunite that man's soul with his glorified and resurrected body.

We need not worry about our loved ones who die in the Lord. They are far more alive than any one of us. They are far better off now than before. For they are in the very presence of him whom to know aright is life everlasting. To be Christians is to have the very hope that when we die, we go into the presence of God.

Does It Hurt to Die?

People often ask: Does it hurt to die? I suppose that really is the fear that we have of death, isn't it? It's not so much the fear of death as it is the fear of dying, the fear of hurting, the fear of the unknown, the fear of walking a path we have never walked before.

The late Donald Grey Barnhouse, a great preacher of the gospel of Jesus Christ, had the sad assignment of laying to rest the wife of his youth while his children were very small. On the way from the service at the church to the burial at the cemetery, his little five-year-old boy looked up into Dr. Barnhouse's eyes and said, "Daddy, did it hurt Mother to die?" The eminent pastor thought his heart would burst within him. What could he say to that little five-year-old that he could understand?

About that time they passed a large truck that had pulled to the side of the road to allow the funeral procession to pass. As it did, the body of the truck came between the sun and the car and passed a shadow over the car. Immediately the man of God said, "Son, did you see the shadow that just ran over us?"

The little boy said, "Yes."

The father asked, "Did it hurt?"

The little boy said, "No."

Then Dr. Barnhouse quoted from David, "Yea, though I walk through the valley of the shadow of death, I will fear no evil: for thou art with me" (Ps. 23:4).

Death to the Christian is like that. It is a shadow that passes over for a moment but then gives way forever to the glorious light of

God's Son. It does not hurt to die; it hurts to live. It hurts to struggle for breath when your lungs are no longer sound as once they were. It hurts to struggle against the difficulty of life, against disease and pain. But it does not hurt to die. Death, for the Christian, is a release into a painless life with Christ.

Will Death Win Forever?

Finally, I wonder if Christian people began to ask Paul: "All right, Paul, we understand that Jesus is coming back and, when he does, that will be the end of all death. We understand that our loved ones will come with him and we'll meet them in the air. And we understand that, in the meantime, they are now in the very presence of our Lord, himself. But what is going to happen in the end? Is death going to be our archenemy forever?"

Paul said that the last enemy to be put under the feet of Jesus is to be the enemy death. It may be the last event of human history, but it shall happen. From that grand resurrection chapter of the Bible, we read:

> *Behold, I shew you a mystery; We shall not all sleep, but we shall all be changed, in a moment, in the twinkling of an eye, at the last trump: for the trumpet shall sound, and the dead shall be raised incorruptible, and we shall be changed. For this corruptible must put on incorruption, and this mortal must put on immortality. So when this corruptible shall have put on incorruption, and this mortal shall have put on immortality, then shall be brought to pass the saying that is written, Death is swallowed up in victory (1 Cor. 15:51–54).*

The bodies of Christians, which lie in the soil, sea, or ashes of God's good earth, shall be changed on that resurrection day. At the end of time, those bodies shall be raised and changed. We shall not all sleep. We shall not all die. Some Christians will still be alive on earth in that day. And even they shall be changed, transformed from the earthly to the heavenly, without passing through the valley of the shadow of death.

THE HOPE OF SEEING JESUS

The apostle Paul, the man of God, stood as it were in the face of death and flaunted his victory in Christ. He baited death; he dared death; he challenged death, "O death, where is thy sting? O grave, where is thy victory? Thanks be unto God, who giveth us the victory through our Lord Jesus Christ."

James Weldon Johnson, black poet and preacher, wrote when a mother died, "Weep not. She is not dead. She's resting in the bosom of Jesus."

"Death, I dare you," Paul as much as said. "What can you do to me?" We think that the worst thing that can happen to a man is for him to die. But the worst that death can do to any man who knows Jesus is to take him and lay him tenderly in the loving arms of Jesus.

That is our hope and no other. And to all who have to pass this way, the Scriptures say, "Therefore, my beloved brethren, be ye steadfast, unmoveable, always abounding in the work of the Lord, forasmuch as ye know that your labour is not in vain in the Lord."

May God put his arms around the family which faces the great intruder, Death. May they feel the warmth and comfort of the presence of Jesus. May they hide in their hearts these words of hope which come from the Book of God. May the hope of seeing Jesus face to face take off the terrible mask of death and show him to be, to the child of God, only the doorkeeper of everlasting life, waiting to usher us into the living presence of our loving Lord.

> Face to face with Christ, my Savior,
> Face to face—what will it be,
> When with rapture I behold him,
> Jesus Christ who died for me!
>
> Face to face I shall behold him,
> Far beyond the starry sky;
> Face to face in all his glory,
> I shall see him by and by!

—CARRIE E. BRECK

14.
The Way Paul Looked at Death
Walter G. Nunn

(A funeral meditation for a devoted Christian)

Once again we face the stark reality of death. This is never easy to do, but it is necessary. For, you see, death is a part of the warp and woof of life.

How shall we look upon death today?

Maybe you view it as an interloper, intruding into your life and into the life of our loved one and friend at a most inopportune time. You feel that death came and cut this person down when he was at the height of his service for God and mankind.

Or perhaps you look upon death as a mystery whose deep, dark secrets you cannot fathom. Of course, there is a mysterious facet about death. We will never understand all there is about it.

Or maybe death to you is an enemy to be shunned at all costs. The New Testament does speak of death as being the last enemy to be destroyed by Jesus Christ. But in some ways death can be a friend. After all, there are many things worse than death.

Although in some ways death is an intruder, a mystery, and an enemy, I would rather think of it the way the apostle Paul did. In Philippians 1:21 he said, "For to me to live is Christ, and to die is gain." Paul was saying that his philosophy of life is that real life and Christ are one and the same. To have abundant life is to have Jesus Christ. To have Christ is to have abundant life.

Can anything beat that? Paul said one thing can: death! Because death is gain. Or as Taylor put it in *The Living Bible:* "And dying—well, that is better yet!"

THE WAY PAUL LOOKED AT DEATH

We could spend our time speaking about what we gain at death, but I would rather tell you why I believe Paul looked upon death as gain.

As we analyze what Paul had to say, there are several figures of speech which he used to describe death that tell us a great deal about it.

First, according to Paul, death means falling asleep in Jesus. In 1 Thessalonians 4:14 we read, "For if we believe that Jesus died and rose again, even so them also which sleep in Jesus will God bring with him."

On one occasion, Jesus spoke of a young girl who had died in this way: "[She] is not dead but sleeping" (Mark 5:39, RSV).

This does not mean that our loved one and friend is unconscious, because actually he is more alert and more awake and more alive than he has ever been. But it does mean that just as we lie down at night to rest in sleep, our loved one and friend now is resting from his labors on earth.

One great writer has compared death to retiring at night and awaking the next morning with another day's task. This suggests to us that our loved one and friend has another task in which he is busily engaged.

In the second place, Paul looked upon death as moving from a tent to a house not made with hands. In 2 Corinthians 5:1 we read, "For we know that if our earthly house of this tabernacle were dissolved, we have a building of God, an house not made with hands, eternal in the heavens." Paul was simply saying that death, among other things, means that we move from a body that is temporary into one that is permanent, a resurrection body that is eternal.

The body in which our loved one and friend lived on this earth was subject to limitations, disease, pain, and death. When Christ returns and we experience a bodily resurrection, our loved one and friend will have a body which is immortal and incorruptible, a new body which can be identified. You will know him in heaven.

Again, the apostle Paul looked at death as the falling in battle of a great warrior. Just before his death he said, "I have fought a good fight" (2 Tim. 4:7).

Let's face it: Life is a struggle, a conflict, a war. The Christian is always engaged in a struggle with the world, the flesh, and the devil. This was true of our loved one and friend. But now all this is ended and there is no more struggle for him.

According to Paul, again, death is an offering to God. In 2 Timothy 4:6, he said, "For I am now ready to be offered." I think this is a very mature concept of death: to look upon death as an offering of oneself to God. And this our loved one and friend has done. He had made a great offering to God: the offering of his life. And now his life is in God's hands.

Paul also looked at death as the departure on a journey to be with Christ. He said, "The time of my departure is at hand"(2 Tim. 4:6). Paul knew that his death was imminent, and he looked upon it as an exodus. On the mount of transfiguration, Jesus thought about his death as an exodus. Ordinarily we think about an exodus not only as a departure, but also as an experience which brings deliverance and freedom. This is what the Exodus means in the Old Testament. The people of God gained deliverance and freedom by leaving Egypt and going into the Promised Land.

Our loved one and friend began this journey in life many years ago. Many of these years he has spent in fellowship with Christ. It has been a journey walked hand in hand and step by step with Christ. And now our loved one and friend is with Christ. At last he has arrived at the destination toward which he has been traveling for many years.

The finishing of a race is another figure of speech which Paul used to describe death. He said, "I have finished my course"(2 Tim. 4:7). Life is not only a battle to be fought, it is a race to be run. Our friend and loved one has run a good race, and he has finished

THE WAY PAUL LOOKED AT DEATH

the race because he has done what God called him to do, and what God wanted him to do. Now the race is over.

Finally, Paul looked upon death as a time when the Christian will receive a reward. In 2 Timothy 4:8, he said, "Henceforth there is laid up for me a crown of righteousness, which the Lord, the righteous judge, shall give me at that day: and not to me only, but unto all them also that love his appearing."

Heaven is a gift, just as salvation is a gift, based upon God's grace and our faith. But in heaven there are varying degrees of rewards, and these rewards are based upon our degree of faithfulness to Christ on this earth. And our loved one and friend has many rewards because of his faithfulness to Christ. We do not know the exact nature of these rewards, but maybe heaven means more to him because he has a greater capacity for it through his faithfulness to Christ.

There are two closing ideas that I want to leave with you. The first comes from the life of Dwight L. Moody who said, "One day you are going to read my obituary in the newspaper. It is going to say that Dwight L. Moody is dead. Do not believe this, because I will be more alive than I have ever been."

Our loved one and friend is more alive now than he has ever been.

The other comes from the life of the late Peter Marshall. As he was being carried on the stretcher from their home to the hospital, after he had suffered a heart attack, he told his wife, Catherine, "Darling, I'll see you in the morning." He thought, of course, that he would see her within a few hours. He did not realize that the truth was he would see her again in the morning of the resurrection.

Do not despair. You will see your loved one again when Christ returns and when all who are deceased in Christ experience the resurrection of the body.

15.
The Hands of Death Are Beautiful
R. Y. Bradford

The apostle Paul, in letters both to the Roman and to the Corinthian Christians, referred to the sufferings, pains, and anguish of life, not of death. Too often we forget that our sorrows and disappointments are the products of life—not of death.

> *For I reckon that the sufferings of this present time are not worthy to be compared with the glory which shall be revealed in us. For the earnest expectation of the creature waiteth for the manifestation of the sons of God. For the creature was made subject to vanity, not willingly, but by reason of him who hath subjected the same in hope. Because the creature itself also shall be delivered from the bondage of corruption into the glorious liberty of the children of God. For we know that the whole creation groaneth and travaileth in pain together until now. And not only they, but ourselves also, which have the first-fruits of the Spirit, even we ourselves groan within ourselves, waiting for the adoption, to wit, the redemption of the body (Rom. 8:18–23).*
>
> *For in this [life] we groan, earnestly desiring to be clothed upon with our house which is from heaven (2 Cor. 5:2).*

We usually speak of death as the Grim Reaper or the Mysterious Dragon that sweeps down into our lives and our homes as our worst enemy. Yet death is often that act of God's mercy that delivers us from the bondages of this life. There comes a time when the hands of death are beautiful!

A poet unknown to me has expressed these truths:

THE HANDS OF DEATH ARE BEAUTIFUL

> Why be afraid of death as though your life was breath!
> Death but anoints your eyes with clay, O glad surprise!
> and
> This is the death of Death to breathe away a breath
> And know the end of strife and taste the deathless life.

A philosopher has said, "It is as natural to die as to be born. On the day of birth man incurs a debt of which death is the payment. The price of life is death."

Always to look on death as an enemy is not in harmony with the Christian philosophy nor the experiences of the multitudes of Christians who have found release from the burdens of this life through the hands of death.

The Hands of Death Are Beautiful—when they are the only hands that can stop the ravages of disease and suffering.

Though science has provided us with pain-decreasing sedatives and many miracle drugs, all of us have seen the conquering march of disease and injury continue until the hands of death in merciful kindness reached forth to stop the disease and suffering. We had prayed for some miracle of science, some kind touch of a friend, or the skilled hands of the doctor to turn back these enemies of our bodies. But only the hands of death answered our prayers. Could such hands be less than beautiful?

The Hands of Death Are Beautiful—when they are the only hands that can close the eyes in restful sleep.

The Scriptures speak of death as a state of both "rest" and "sleep." Many times have we heard the sighs and cries of the afflicted as they sought a time of restful sleep. But all that the hands of loved ones and friends could do was only useless effort. Only by the hands of death could the burdens of life, the pains of the body, the concerns of the mind and anguishes of the heart be lifted and laid aside so that we could say, "He is asleep," or "She is at rest." Surely hands that can minister to our loved ones, bringing peace and rest in the time of their greatest need, must be beautiful. These are not the long ugly hands we see depicted as the hands of death.

The Hands of Death Are Beautiful—when they draw the shades on the eventide of life and swing open the doors of life eternal.

However beautiful life has been, the close of it cannot be altered. Who is the person so wise as to be able to say, "Now is the time," or "You have lived long enough"? None of us is so wise.

Only the hands of death can skillfully bring to the close a beautiful life. Only these hands can begin to harvest the fruits that are to bless the world until Christ comes to claim his own. Do we know of any other hands that hold the keys that unlock the door to the dawn of God's eternity? Search across the land; you will find no other hands holding this key to the city with streets of gold.

An unknown poet shows that he understands that experience.

> Thy day has come and gone;
> Thy sun has risen, not set;
> Thy life is now beyond
> The reach of death or change,
>   Not ended—but begun.
> O noble soul! O gentle heart!
>   Hail, and farewell.

16.
Slipping the Bonds of Earth
Mahan Siler, Jr.

> *(The following meditation was part of a memorial service for a young man killed in Vietnam. A piece of sculpture representing a cluster of doves in flight was placed within the church building as a symbol of his life and witness.)*

Doves in flight . . . doves beginning to fly . . . and D. S. We remember with both sadness and celebration our son, our brother, our fellow believer, our friend.

These sculptured birds appear to be early in flight. So was D. His adulthood was barely launched. His flight of manhood was just off the ground . . . then so abruptly interrupted!

You remember him as a boy when his wings were developing; I knew him, with you, as a young man when his wings were fully developed, yet untried. Or better, we witnessed his attempts to fly, only to see the false starts and restless floundering around on the ground.

Yet when he was shot down in Vietnam, he was in flight. His letters to family and friends conveyed purpose and confidence and human courage unknown to him during his adolescent years among us. Clearly, he was feeling the power of his own wings against the winds of stress. That precisely is a point of much pain today. What sadness! To see a man struck down when the flight of maturity had just begun. We are in touch with that anguish as we gather to remember him with honor. Now this sadness tempers the anger—that former outrage over witnessing such potential flowering suddenly nipped in the bud.

The covey of birds suggests another felt truth. D. S. did not fly alone, nor did he die alone. Vietnam witnessed the untimely death of many young men. His letters reflected his bewilderment as he risked his life along with others in a war with unclear causes and unclear support and unclear goals. This sculptured covey of birds, frozen and therefore incomplete in flight, holds before us the corporate anguish of that war.

Look again, these birds are doves. The dove is the biblical symbol for the Holy Spirit . . . the Holy Spirit of peace . . . the living breath of God's *Shalom.*

D. was becoming a man of peace, feeling out-of-joint in a land and time of violence. The dove was in his sight, hovering close to his hellish experience. From those with him in his last days, we received the news that he died at peace within himself, with God, even with those responsible for the war.

So the first word felt—the word that caused us to gather—was the word *death.* We come together in remembrance of D. because he died. Yet the last word that rings from both his life and this symbol is not death, but life—not war, but peace—not despair, but hope. Those precious words will never again be so glibly shaped by our lips. His life, a part of the life-giving love of our Lord, gives depth to the words: life, peace, hope. These jewels we hold with fresh appreciation as we claim afresh the privilege no longer his—namely, to continue in the flight of our Christlike becoming.

> Oh, I have slipped the surly bonds of earth
> And danced the skies . . .
> . . . .
> The high, untrespassed sanctity of space,
> Put out my hand and touched the face of God.
>
> —John G. Magee, Jr.

17.
What Is the Color of Death?
W. Ches Smith, III

We come today as little children—death makes us so. It always does. We are grateful for all that medical science has done, and is doing, for our good and for the benefit of mankind. But medical science, at it's best, is not enough to stay the hand of death. Coming together today as little children is good; little children are teachable, and we need to learn in this experience.

In recent years, many children's books have been published in which instructions are given to color the house brown, the tree green, and the sky blue. We come today as little children, and we are to color this experience of death. Color it we must, but most important is how we color it!

First, we will color it *grief*. It's neither wrong nor inappropriate to grieve. This makes us human—it proves that we loved. Sadness and brokenheartedness are not to be denied. Jesus wept at the death of a dear friend. He was deeply moved as he stood by the grave of Lazarus. He wept with Mary and Martha, whose hearts were broken over their brother's death.

Grief is part and parcel of life. Grief is wholesome. It marks the difference between man and the beasts of the field and the fowl of the air. Grief is found in the texture of time. Artists would be at a loss to paint without the dark colors for shadows and contrast. It is impossible to live and love without grief. It is impossible to grow and mature without it. Robert Browning Hamilton was right when he wrote:

> I walked a mile with Pleasure,
>   She chatted me all the way.
> But I was none the wiser
>   For what she had to say.
>
> I walked a mile with sorrow
>   And ne'er a word said she,
> But oh, the things I learned from her
>   When sorrow walked with me.

Second, we will color it *gratitude*. The noblest of all virtues is gratitude. Thankfulness is next to godliness. It is easy to give thanks to God when the sun is shining and everything is going our way. But what if we don't see the sun? One piece of wood is as good as the next until you put stress upon it. One piece of rope is as strong as the next until tension is applied to it. One life is as good as the next until a heavy load is placed upon it. It is then that you fully see the character of a person.

We ought to be grateful for every opportunity to carry heavy loads, to climb steep hills or to walk through dark valleys, for this can demonstrate one's finest qualities.

The apostle Paul prayed at first that his "thorn in the flesh" might be removed. God said, "No, you will not be the kind of man I need you to be without the weight and agony of this burden. We will leaven it and together we will show the world what can be done." In the end, Paul rejoiced with thanksgiving for that thorn, and for the privilege of giving an example of faith and trust.

Third, we will color this experience *God*. The only right relationship we can have with God is one of dependency. "Unless ye become as little children" Christ said. We are his children, and we can depend upon God to do what is right and best for us. This is what the apostle Paul was saying to the Christians in Rome: God is at work in all things for the good of those who trust him and love him (Rom. 8:28).

We may not understand all that God is doing. In the time of death, we may be in the dark as to the timing of this experience and the circumstances under which it happens. But we can know that God is at work and that it is important for us to cooperate with him.

Finally, we will color this experience *gone*. Perhaps, the most important aspect of death is for us to be aware that our friend or loved one or companion is gone. No amount of superficial camouflage will conceal this fact or lessen its blow. Death takes away that which we love dearly and long to hold to us closely.

Remember what Jesus said: "Let not your heart be troubled: ye believe in God, believe also in me. In my Father's house are many mansions: if it were not so, I would have told you. I go to prepare a place for you" (John 14:1-2). That's right! Jesus has gone to prepare a place for everyone who believes that he is the way, the truth, and the life, and that no one can get to the Father's house except through him.

Jesus has gone ahead, but he has not forgotten us. He said, "I will never leave thee, nor forsake thee" (Heb. 13:5). He promised, "I go to prepare a place for you . . . . I will come again, and receive you unto myself; that where I am"—that's where *you* will be! The Bible says when we are absent from the body we are present with the Lord.

Dark colors and bright colors—but in the end, the shining light of heaven and the glory of God.

What is the color of death? You cannot escape coloring this experience with your own thoughts and emotions. The important question is, *How* will you color it?

Unrelieved grief? Or gilded with the hope in God through Jesus Christ.

Suggested Scripture Readings: John 14:1-6; Romans 8:14-18,28-39.

18.
When Is a Man Ready to Die?
Richard Jackson

All of life is filled with preparation. Every day men are found in the midst of some type of making ready. Yet many persons, strangely, spend most of their time making preparation to live on and on. Even though life obviously is fleeting, they act as if it were forever. While we see about us the uncertainty of earthly existence and the evidence that death is the ultimate end of it, still some live as though life were forever and death will come never.

Days pass into weeks very swiftly, and weeks into years. Year after year people go on amassing possessions and attaining positions in order to have the luxuries of life and to gain high esteem in the eyes of others. Many a man will spend all his adult life working toward the time of retirement and make many provisions for that prospect of physical rest. Yet few take time to make proper preparation for the rest that is eternal.

Surely life is to be desired. We want to experience it to its fullest. It is fitting for men to apply themselves in toil and expend God-given talents and energies to live life to its utmost. But what is life at its best? Is it years without sickness? Is it avoidance of physical pain? Is it the assurance of financial security? All of these go to make life a bit more pleasant. With all these lovely features, however, life does not approach its intended completion.

Life without proper spiritual alignment is scarcely worth the effort, for men were not created to live in the grip of sin and Satan. All about us, many go on and on, getting rather than giving, luring rather than loving, seeking and never finding. They spend their days seeking to make a living and failing to find life.

The only preparation for living that is worthwhile is a decision of faith in the Lord Jesus Christ.

When is a person ready to die? The answer to that lies in the answer to another question: When is a person really living? Man really lives only when he comes to know Jesus Christ as his personal Lord and Savior. To know Jesus Christ gives one eternal life. To have eternal life prepares one for physical death.

"I am the resurrection, and the life," Jesus said. "He that liveth and believeth in me, though he were dead, yet shall he live: and whosoever liveth and believeth in me shall never die" (John 11:25-26). To know Jesus Christ and to possess eternal life in him brings one to the genuine experience of living. This experience of life prepares us for a victorious experience of death.

While some men plan to live forever, wise men prepare to die. Death is inevitable; it is appointed unto men once to die. "For what is your life?" The Scriptures state that "It is even a vapour that appeareth for a little time, and then vanisheth away" (Jas. 4:14).

How is one to come to this Jesus who is the resurrection and the life?

There are many good and reasonable ways to prepare for death physically. That preparation which comes through a proper relation to one's family is good. The foresightedness to take care of financial things through insurance and estate planning is wonderful. Even the purchasing of burial lots and the provision for a funeral are significant.

There are many things that go into making one ready for death as a physical experience, but there is only one adequate preparation for death spiritually. Church membership and baptism, as good as they are, are not sufficient. Good clean moral living is certainly not enough. The only provision for death which is complete is following the scriptural teaching of faith in Jesus Christ.

In the Scriptures, there is recorded the story of a man who was ready to die. His name was Simeon and we read about him in Luke 2. The Bible says of Simeon that he was "a just man and devout." He was controlled by the Spirit of God and lived in anticipation of the coming of the Lord Christ. Simeon had a promise from God that he should not taste death until he had the wonderful privilege of seeing God's Messiah. When Jesus' mother and her husband brought the Baby up to the Temple to present him according to the custom of the Jews, the Bible says, Simeon recognized the fulfillment of God's promise and actually prayed for his own death.

"Lord, now let thy servant depart in peace," he prayed. How could Simeon offer that kind of petition? Only because he had learned how to live; therefore, he was ready to die.

By looking at Simeon's life, we see that he was ready to die because he had believed the Word of God. In Luke 2:25–26, we read that Simeon had studied and knew the words of prophecy. He believed the written Word of God and he believed the word of God that had been revealed to him by the Holy Spirit. When we think in terms of death, particularly, it is my firm conviction that no other book and no other word has any kind of comfort or source of strength except the eternal Word of the living God.

No other philosopher has ever dared suggest an answer to death. No other intellectual discipline has ever claimed to have a sufficient solution. Only the Word of God clearly and plainly gives us directions and descriptions of eternal life. Only our Lord Christ, God's living Word, has been able to claim "I am the resurrection and the life."

A man has no adequate preparation for life or for death except that which comes from reading and accepting and believing the Word of God. If a person refuses the Bible and its revelation, then I have no other hope to offer him that will take him through the hour of death. There is no other source of comfort.

WHEN IS A MAN READY TO DIE?

We have been told that when Sir Walter Raleigh lay near death, he called his son-in-law to his side and said, "Son bring me the Book."

Perplexed, and knowing a vast library was available, the young man asked, "Sir, what book, which book?"

"Son, there is but one Book," Sir Walter Raleigh responded, "Bring me The Book!"

When a man approaches death, there is only one book that contains the words of life. A man is ready to die only after he has come to believe the Word of God.

Simeon was ready to die when he had seen the salvation of God in Christ. He took the baby Jesus up in his arms and prayed that he might depart in peace, "For mine eyes have seen thy salvation" (Luke 2:30).

The Bible is a book of redeeming grace; salvation is its center and redemption is its very reason for being. The Bible tells us that God in love reached out to save man from his sin. A person never comes to know life until he has come to the salvation of God which is in Jesus Christ. A person is never ready for death until he stands in that saving Life.

There is no way someone else can prepare for your death or for mine. Death is an individual thing that each of us must face personally. Preparation for death must be individual and personal. The Bible says, "Whosoever shall call upon the name of the Lord shall be saved" (Acts 2:21). No person is ready to die until he, like Simeon, has seen the salvation of the Lord.

Finally, we learn from Simeon's experience that a person is ready to die only after he has given witness of his faith in that Savior who is Jesus Christ. It is beautiful in the Gospel of Luke where Simeon took the Baby up in his arms and testified before all the people.

They must have thought the quaint old man had become senile. Holding a tiny baby in his arms, he was talking about a

Savior, a Messiah. The Jews all expected a Messiah. They knew they needed a deliverer, but they thought surely he would come riding on a magnificent horse and wearing a warrior's armor.

The spectators must have thought, *How could old Simeon have grown so feeble and doting to believe this child of peasant parents could be God's Messiah?* Yet Simeon, with no fear of what they thought, with a calm faith in his soul, lifted up Jesus, testifying that this Child was indeed the Lord's Christ.

Since then, many people have come to death without ever having testified of finding life in Christ. Maybe deep within some souls there was a saving faith, even though it was not well expressed. Doubt always lingers in such a situation.

Without a testimony, a person is never really ready to die. There can never be a testimony shared at his funeral until he has had a testimony expressed in his life. Through the life that one has lived and through the words that he has spoken, he gives faithful witness to the salvation he has in Jesus Christ.

No one can live as God would have him live in Jesus until he unashamedly and openly stands to testify of his faith in Jesus as his personal Savior.

The most important preparation for life is spiritual preparation and the only preparation for death is having come to know life which is eternal. There is only one way to live, and that is in the Lord. There is really only one way to die, and that is in the Lord.

Are you prepared? Are you sure that eternal home is ready to welcome you? Life is available, life is unbroken and unending, life in Jesus Christ. Would you, with Simeon, make preparation so that you can say, "I am ready to die because I have learned to live through faith in Jesus Christ"?

19.
Not Why, But How
Charles E. Harvey

2 Corinthians 1:1–11

Sorrow, trials, tribulations seem to be inevitable experiences of life. One does not live long without encountering adversity in some fashion and to some degree. Each day we are reminded of these realities as we read of their occurrence in the lives of those we do not know. However, we often refuse to admit the possibility of sorrow invading our own personal realm. Sooner or later, probability becomes inevitability and sadness becomes part of our experience.

No one, not even the child of God, is exempt from facing the reality of death in his own life or death among his dearest loved ones. Christians are not promised deliverance from these dark hours. God does promise strength and grace sufficient to encounter and to win victory within these experiences.

David realized that faith does not bring immunity from sorrow. "Yea, though I walk through the valley of the shadow of death," he wrote (Ps. 23:4). The phrase could be interpreted, "Yea, *when* I walk . . . ." He claimed the only promise he knew—the presence of God.

Paul wrote lucidly and candidly about suffering in the life of the Christian: "For I reckon that the sufferings of this present time are not worthy to be compared with the glory which shall be revealed in us" (Rom. 8:18).

Much of the tragedy which comes to us we are not able to understand. Naturally, the old question Why? accompanies almost every sorrow. If we could understand everything, we would be equal with God. Our children cannot understand us, but it is at that point that the relationship of parent-child is validated. Our inability to comprehend every sorrow establishes the validity of God's existence and our relationship to him. What great comfort to accept the fact that he knows best!

The mature Christian will ask How? instead of Why? Every tragedy is not good, but we can let God bring good from it. To the Corinthian Christians, Paul listed three ways in which sorrow could be used to enrich our lives and the lives of our friends.

We Are Qualified to Comfort Others

"Blessed be God," Paul wrote, "even the Father of our Lord Jesus Christ, the Father of mercies, and the God of all comfort; who comforteth us in all our tribulation, that we may be able to comfort them which are in any trouble, by the comfort wherewith we ourselves are comforted of God" (2 Cor. 1:3–4). Our God is recognized as the God of all comfort. He does not comfort in the sense that we feel no sense of loss. The comfort which he provides is encouragement; an enabling Presence brings hope and heart to the Christian. This personal experience of the Christian qualifies him confidently to comfort those who pass through a similar experience.

One young couple's son died early in life, a young man who was preparing for the ministry. They never understood, but they found comfort and encouragement in God during the dark hours of their grief. God's Presence in that experience equipped them to dispense comfort to countless others who suffered a similar loss.

We may not be able to understand the sorrows of life, but we do know how they can be transformed into blessings.

We Learn to Not Trust in Ourselves

"But we had the sentence of death in ourselves," Paul wrote, "that we should not trust in ourselves, but in God which raiseth the dead" (2 Cor. 1:9). His reference to the affliction or pressure which he experienced in Asia does not reveal its nature. It could have been mental or physical suffering. The depth of his suffering is the major emphasis, "that we were pressed out of measure, above strength, insomuch that we despaired even of life" (2 Cor. 1:8).

This intense suffering taught Paul a great lesson. Probably he was already aware of his need to rely upon God wholly, but this experience quickened his conviction that his human resources were inadequate. Whatever his dependence on God before the experience, it seemed to be minor compared to the complete dependence which he learned in Asia.

Sometimes, we become victims of our own affluent society. Science and technology have brought such progress that the spirit of man has become one of independence rather than dependence. We often feel capable of handling life's situations in our own strength and wisdom. This illusion of self-sufficiency is soon torn apart by difficult experiences which reveal our inadequacy of wisdom and insufficiency of strength. We are driven to rely not on ourselves, but on God.

We Can Enter the Ministry of Prayer

"Ye also helping together by prayer for us," Paul wrote, "that for the gift bestowed upon us by the means of many persons thanks may be given by many on our behalf" (2 Cor. 1:11). Paul was saying that the prayers of his friends brought to him a sense of security. He believed that their prayers contributed in some way to his deliverance by God.

Our friends respond to our needs in a time of sorrow more quickly than at any other time. We need them in such an hour. Their ministry is invaluable to us. Expressions of sympathy and concern serve to alleviate some of the hurt and loneliness created with the passing of a loved one. However, the prayers of our Christian friends serve to strengthen us beyond our understanding and comprehension.

Today our prayer is that, when we leave this service of memorial, our friends will be more sensitive than ever before to the presence of God and his enabling grace. Let us take refuge in all the promises of God and rejoice in all the provisions that only God could make for loved ones. May we commit ourselves anew to the fulfillment of his will and purpose for our lives.

20.
I Believe in Immortality
James P. Wesberry

In Elmwood Cemetery stands a monument marking the spot near my boyhood home and church where I expect someday to be buried. To me it is most beautiful, not for its bright white Georgia marble but for its meaning and message.

The marble shaft tapers into sections as it stands over seven feet tall, pointing to the greatness of God. In the middle of the monument is a wreath of lilies. The lily has ever been the emblem of resurrection. In and through the wreath is a cross, which of course symbolizes the death of the Lord Jesus Christ for our sins. In the middle of the cross, on an open Bible are three words which summarize our faith: CHRIST OUR HOPE. Christ is indeed our hope in this life, in death, and in the world to come—our only hope for time and eternity.

Beneath the wreath and deeply carved into the marble are these words of the apostle Paul: "Our Saviour Jesus Christ, . . . hath abolished death, and hath brought life and immortality to light through the gospel" (2 Tim. 1:10). This verse summarizes my faith in immortality. I could find no more suitable text to convey to future generations my undying faith in Jesus Christ and in the wonderful truth that he has abolished death for those who trust in him.

On several occasions, it has been my happy and thrilling experience to visit the little town of Bethany just outside the city of Jerusalem. There one finds a comparatively new, beautiful church known as the Church of Lazarus. Nearby is his ancient tomb. You will recall that Lazarus had been dead for four days when Jesus called him back to life.

On one of my visits there, I found an old man keeping the tomb whose name also was Lazarus. He conducted us down the narrow stairway into the dark grave below, holding in his hand a tiny, flickering candle, whose rays gave us light to enter the tomb.

This, my friends, is what Jesus does for us. He sheds into the grave, not the rays of flickering candlelight, but the powerful searchlight of his gospel. He abolished death and illuminated immortality.

Perhaps it sounds strange to speak of death and then to say there is no death. But all who have put their faith in our great Savior Jesus Christ know that this is true.

John Luckey McCreery, in his beautiful poem, "There Is No Death," proclaimed this most positively when he penned these lines:

> There is no death! the stars go down
>   To rise upon some other shore;
> And bright in heaven's jeweled crown
>   They shine forevermore.
>
> There is no death! the forest leaves
>   Convert to life the viewless air;
> The rocks disorganize to feed
>   The hungry moss they bear.
>
> There is no death! the dust we tread
>   Shall change beneath the summer showers
> To golden grain, or mellow fruit,
>   Or rainbow-tinted flowers.
>
> And ever near us, though unseen,
>   The dear immortal spirits tread;
> For all the boundless universe
>   Is life—there are no dead.

Another poet has expressed uniquely the negative side of this

I BELIEVE IN IMMORTALITY

question. McCreery said positively, "There is no death," and another, taking a long look at death, asks, "If Life Were All."

> If life were all, and death its certain end,
> If nothing lured the soul to higher aims,
> If what we cherish here and guard and tend,
> Were crown and summit of all life attains,
> Rewards so small had scarce repaid
>   the battle life sustains
> If life were all.
>
> Were there no faith that on another shore
> Beyond the distance of this life's utmost scope
> Lay Beulah lands, where joy reigns ever more,
> Surpassing all things that hearts may hope
> Beneath life's pall it were not well,
>   for these vain years to grope
> If life were all.
>
> If life were all, and amid its wild alarms
> No cross, no blood shone through its awful years,
> If through its darkness no outstretched arms,
> Beckoned the woeful forsake his fears
> O cup of gall; life were not worth
>   its floodtide of tears
> If life were all.

Yet if this life really ended all, I believe it would still be worthwhile to live it for Jesus. If there were no hereafter, I'd certainly want to be a Christian, anyway. But, thank God, this life does not end all.

Psychiatrists and psychologists are telling us so. In *Newsweek*, July 12, 1976, an article called "Life After Death" tells how a patient who had been pronounced dead, unexpectedly revived later, described what happened to him during that time when his body exhibited no signs of life.

He became aware of other presences in the room and gradually he was drawn to a vague "being of light," with whom he longed to stay and only reluctantly came back into his physical body. One of the researchers said that she now has proof that there is "life after death" on the basis of hundreds of such stories. Death, she says, brought to these people such a feeling of hope and peace that not one of them was afraid to die again.

These documented accounts about what happens after death are interesting. But my faith in life beyond the grave is not based on what researchers say. It is based on what Jesus said. He is the final authority on life, death, and immortality. Another unknown poet has expressed it in this way:

> Think of stepping on shore and finding it Heaven,
> Of taking hold of a hand, and finding it God's hand,
> Of breathing a new air and finding it celestial air.
> Of feeling invigorated and finding it immortality,
> Of passing from storm and tempest to an unknown calm,
> Of waking up and finding it Home!

My friends, for the Christian, *this* is dying!

Perhaps you recall the beautiful friendship of Alfred Tennyson and Arthur Hallam. When Hallam died, Tennyson wrote a beautiful poem entitled "In Memoriam," in which he showed that a flaming spirit like Arthur Hallam's could not be quenched and the bond of love between them could not be extinguished. "Endless love," Tennyson said, "implies endless living."

> My own dim life should teach me this,
> That life shall live for evermore,
> Else earth is darkness at the core,
> And dust and ashes all that is.

The poet went on to describe death as "sunset," "evening star," "twilight," "evening bell," and "after that the dark."

What could be more beautiful than a gold and crimson sunset? But sunset is only the reflection of a far vaster beauty—it is cloud-reflected light from the hidden sun. The beauty of life's sunset is the revelation of the greater life of the unseen Son shining more radiantly on another shore.

For the Christian, death is not sundown, it is sunup. It is not darkness, but light; not gloom, but glory. Death can be our friend; not an end, but a beginning; not an exit, but an entrance; not annihilation, but everlasting life. It is "transplanted human worth that blooms to profit otherwhere." Death is not, as Shelley said, "lying down on the lone couch of everlasting sleep," but rising up to walk all over God's heaven.

I believe in our Savior's gospel of the divine fatherhood. Jesus taught us that God is our Father and that he is a good father. We can trust our loved ones in his hands. He knows what is best for them. It is the instinct of fatherhood to create, protect, and prolong life. A God of love gives immortality to those whom he makes in his own image.

If God has no more purpose for us then to plow us under to make room for oncoming generations, then it would seem that he is more of a wholesale farmer than he is a Father who loves his children. He who is immortal love gives those he loves immortal life.

John Greenleaf Whittier, in his poem, "The Eternal Goodness," is right:

> Yet, in the maddening maze of things,
>   And tossed by storm and flood,
> To one fixed trust my spirit clings:
>   I know that God is good!
>
> ....
> I know not where His islands lift
>   Their fronded palms in air;
> I only know I cannot drift
>   Beyond His love and care.

Jesus never argued immortality, he declared it. He promised it to his disciples: "I give unto them eternal life; and they shall never perish" (John 10:28). He also said, "I am the resurrection, and the life: he that believeth in me, though he were dead, yet shall he live: And whosoever liveth and believeth in me shall never die" (John 11:25). Let us underscore those words, *"shall never die"!*

Apart from Jesus, our fairest hopes and fondest dreams pass into an all-engulfing night, but clasping him by faith, we clasp "heaven's glad forever midst earth's little while." If it were not for Jesus, we could never see beyond the veil of death.

Christ brought immortality to light in the gospel of his miraculous incarnation. The shadow of the cross fell upon his cradle. The doctrines of incarnation, redemption, and resurrection are closely interwoven. Christ did not become flesh to live among people who were to be annihilated. Our Lord's death on the cross was not for creatures on their way to dust, but for spirits who must presently meet God. His sacrifice had eternity and infinity in it.

I believe in immortality because when I visit the Garden Tomb in Jerusalem I find quite a difference between his grave and all the other thousands of graves I have visited across the world. His is an empty grave. "He is not here," said the angel, "Come, see the place where the Lord lay" (Matt. 28:6). What a difference the grammar makes! Glorious is the grammar of Easter morning: it was "where he lay," not "where he lies," that transformed the world. Christ is evermore alive and because he lives, "we too shall live."

Immortality thus illuminated becomes God's summons to all of us to repent and obey the gospel. It compels us to view our sins under the aspects of eternity. In the light of immortality, sin can no longer be regarded as a mere trifle or superficial strain, but as a crime against Almighty God.

When we are brought face to face with the fact that we are going to live forever, our little day on earth takes on new meaning and is invested with new value. Seeing that every bit of good we do in this world lives on, let us seek to live well. Seeing that we are building for eternity, let us seek to live noble and worthy lives, to be faithful to our appointed tasks and true to our responsibilities.

Blessed is that man or woman whose hope is built on Jesus Christ, who has "abolished death" and "brought life and immortality to light through the gospel."

21.
A Choice of Death
Jack P. Lowndes

(Funeral Message for a Suicide)

We come today to pay our respects to the memory of one who lived among us as friend, fellow citizen, and loved one. We cannot help but come to this memorial service in a mood of thoughtfulness. May it also be a mood of understanding. As we seek to understand recent events and the reasons why we are here, we turn to that great source of knowledge and understanding as well as comfort, the Word of God.

First, I read several verses from Psalm 130:

> *Out of the depths have I cried unto thee, O Lord.*
> *Lord, hear my voice: let thine ears be attentive to the voice of my supplications.*
> *If thou, Lord, shouldest mark iniquities, O Lord, who shall stand?*
> *But there is forgiveness with thee, that thou mayest be feared.*
> *Let Israel hope in the Lord: for with the Lord there is mercy, and with him is plenteous redemption (vv. 1–4,7).*

Again, reading Psalm 15:1–2:

> *Lord, who shall abide in thy tabernacle? who shall dwell in thy holy hill?*
> *He that walketh uprightly, and worketh righteousness, and speaketh the truth in his heart.*

As we come today in this memorial service, there are many things that we do not understand. It is always difficult to understand when we are too close to the situation. But in God's time we will know and understand what is now a vast tangle of mystery and loneliness.

One thing we do well to keep in mind is the admonition of Jesus, "Judge not, that ye be not judged" (Matt. 7:1).

Only God can know the sickness and suffering which gripped the mind and spirit of our friend. But we do have the assurance that God does know. Therefore, it is not up to us to judge. While we come to this place in sadness, we can also come in thankfulness for the life that was lived among us.

Looking back over this life that has now so suddenly been cut short, we find much for which to be grateful. We think of all that our friend meant to others, the place he had created for himself in the family circle, and his service to the community, the church, and the world. All of this still stands and we pay tribute to the many ways in which our lives were enriched by his and to his efforts and service, which will be felt for a long time.

As we face the reality of death, there is sadness. We never like to see our loved ones go from us, no matter what the age or the circumstances of death. When they leave, we always miss them. There is always that empty place that no one else can fill. This is especially true as we come to this place today. However, this is true because of love.

It would be a terrible thing if we did not have love and did not miss people when they leave us to go into eternity. And so, today we are grateful for this life, a gift of God to us. And we sorrow at his death. As we come with gratitude, in a nonjudgmental attitude, and in sadness, we come also to proclaim our faith in God, who has revealed himself in Jesus Christ.

In the words of the apostle Paul, "I am persuaded, that neither death, nor life, nor angels, nor principalities, nor powers, nor things present, nor things to come, nor height, nor depth, nor any other creature, shall be able to separate us from the love of God, which is in Christ Jesus our Lord" (Rom. 8:38–39).

This is the promise of our faith. "We know that if the earthly tent we live in is destroyed, we have a building from God, a house not made with hands, eternal in the heavens. For while we are still in this tent, we sigh with anxiety; not that we would be unclothed, but that we would be further clothed, so that what is mortal may be swallowed up by life" (2 Cor. 5:1,4,RSV).

Many times it was my privilege to hear our departed friend express his faith. In life he was faithful to the church, to his family, and to his obligations. I do not understand this present moment, but I do know God; I have confidence and faith in him and his love as it has been revealed in Jesus Christ. God is a God of infinite love and grace. I have confidence that anyone who puts his trust in Jesus Christ will find that God loves with a deep understanding and patience beyond our comprehension. In his eternal kingdom there is a place for all who have claimed forgiveness through acceptance of Jesus Christ as Savior.

Therefore, we express our willingness to commit this "good" man, our friend, to the keeping of a "good" God. Such a person is no stranger to One who, while he surely does not overlook our faults, can be depended upon to care for those who have trusted him for life and forgiveness. Unto the Lord's gracious mercy and protection we commit our friend and loved one.

I close this meditation with the words of John Greenleaf Whittier:

> When on my day of life the night is falling
>   And, in the wind from unsunned spaces blown,
> I hear far voices out of darkness calling
>   My feet to paths unknown;
>
> Thou, who hast made my home of life so pleasant,
>   Leave not its tenant when its walls decay;
> O Love Divine, O Helper ever present,
>   Be Thou my strength and stay . . . .

Suffice it if—my good and ill unreckoned,
  And both forgiven through thy abounding grace—
I find myself by hands familiar beckoned
  Unto my fitting place—

Some humble door among thy many mansions,
  Some sheltering shade where sin and striving cease,
And flows forever through heaven's green expansions
  The river of thy peace.

22.
Graveside Committal Service
Charles G. Fuller

The Scriptures often refer to flowers as a means of graphic illustration. To portray the durability of God's Word, the Bible says, "The grass withers, the flower fades, /but the word of God stands for ever" (Isa. 40:8, RSV).

To symbolize the beautiful but, at best, brief duration of human life, the Bible says, "All flesh is as grass, /and all its beauty is like the flower of the field. /The grass withers, the flower fades (Isa. 40:6–7, RSV).

To express tangibly our love and sympathy at a time like this, we send flowers to those whose hearts are heavy in the loss of their loved one.

And to further use flowers as a means of expression and symbolism, I have chosen these three flowers from among the arrangements about the grave here, sent by loved ones and friends. These three flowers simply but beautifully tell the story of a life as God intended that it be lived and remembered.

The *red flower* is symbolic of the means whereby we start life as God has made it available to us: it symbolizes the *shed blood of Christ,* God's means through which we are born into his family. The Bible teaches us: "Without shedding of blood [there] is no remission [of sin]" (Heb. 9:22).

The *white flower* symbolizes the purity which is ours once we have been placed beneath the blood of Christ and been born anew into God's family. It is as the Bible says: "Though your sins be as scarlet, they shall be as white as snow; though they be red like crimson, they shall be as wool" (Isa. 1:18).

The *golden flower* is symbolic of the high and golden promises of God which are ours to claim *before* eternity and ours to experience *in* eternity.

The highest and most glowing of all the promises of our Lord is the one found in the fourteenth chapter of John's Gospel:

> *Let not your heart be troubled: ye believe in God, believe also in me. In my Father's house are many mansions: if it were not so, I would have told you. I go to prepare a place for you. And if I go and prepare a place for you, I will come again, and receive you unto myself; that where I am, there ye may be also (John 14:1–3).*

So today we lay to rest in the earth a physical house, a tabernacle of flesh. As we do so, we leave here in this place a monument to remind us of a life, a life known and cherished by the loved ones who are gathered here. But we are reminded that the earth is not the *final* resting place for us. It is where we lay the body down but that which gives the body life, the spirit, the inner and "real" us, lives on and on and on.

And it is God's desire that we live on, and on, with him.

It is as Jesus said when he faced the grave he would conquer by his resurrection: "I go to prepare a place for you . . . that where I am, there ye may be also."

23.
Military Graveside Service
Francis Jackson Redford

(The following is a suggested sequence for an abbreviated graveside military service.)

On arrival at the cemetery, the chaplain will lead the procession from the hearse to the grave, reciting slowly and distinctly the twenty-third Psalm:

> The Lord is my shepherd; I shall not want.
> He maketh me to lie down in green pastures: he leadeth me beside the still waters.
> He restoreth my soul: he leadeth me in the paths of righteousness for his name's sake.
> Yea, though I walk through the valley of the shadow of death, I will fear no evil: for thou art with me; thy rod and thy staff they comfort me.
> Thou preparest a table before me in the presence of mine enemies: thou anointest my head with oil; my cup runneth over.
> Surely goodness and mercy shall follow me all the days of my life: and I will dwell in the house of the Lord for ever.

When the casket has been placed over the grave, the pallbearers raise the flag from the casket and hold it waist high in horizontal position throughout the service until the conclusion of taps.

A quartet could then sing, *a capella,* two stanzas of "My Country, 'Tis of Thee."

The chaplain should then read these Scripture passages:

> Now this I say, brethren, that flesh and blood cannot inherit the kingdom of God; neither doth corruption inherit incorruption.

MILITARY GRAVESIDE SERVICE

Behold, I shew you a mystery; We shall not all sleep, but we shall all be changed.

In a moment, in the twinkling of an eye, at the last trump: for the trumpet shall sound, and the dead shall be raised incorruptible, and we shall be changed.

For this corruptible must put on incorruption, and this mortal must put on immortality.

So when this corruptible shall have put on incorruption, and this mortal shall have put on immortality, then shall be brought to pass the saying that is written, Death is swallowed up in victory.

O death, where is thy sting? O grave, where is thy victory?

The sting of death is sin; and the strength of sin is the law.

But thanks be to God, which giveth us the victory through our Lord Jesus Christ.

Therefore, my beloved brethren, be ye steadfast, unmoveable, always abounding in the work of the Lord, forasmuch as ye know that your labour is not in vain in the Lord (1 Cor. 15:50–58).

Jesus said unto her, I am the resurrection, and the life: he that believeth in me, though he were dead, yet shall he live:

And whosoever liveth and believeth in me shall never die (John 11:25–26).

The chaplain should then pray for the bereaved, express gratitude for the blessed hope we have in Christ, and give thanks for the fact that God is near to us in the dark hours of life.

The chaplain should end his prayer by saying, "We ask this in the name of him who taught us to pray,

Our Father which art in heaven, Hallowed be thy name. Thy Kingdom come. Thy will be done in earth, as it is in heaven. Give us this day our daily bread. And forgive us our debts, as we forgive our debtors.

And lead us not into temptation, but deliver us from evil: For Thine is the kingdom, and the power, and the glory, for ever. Amen" (Matt. 6:9–13).

After prayer, all military personnel should come to present arms (except the firing squad and pallbearers). Civilians should place their hats or hands over their hearts during the firing and sounding of taps.

The firing squad then fires three volleys.

The firing squad then comes to present arms.

The bugler immediately sounds taps.

At the conclusion of taps, the rifles of the firing squad are locked.

The flag is then folded and presented to the next of kin.

The chaplain then pronounces the benediction:

> *The Lord bless thee, and keep thee:*
> *The Lord make his face shine upon thee, and be gracious unto thee:*
> *The Lord lift up his countenance upon thee, and give thee peace (Num. 6:24–26).*

In Jesus' name. Amen.

Part IV

The Bible and Grief

24.
Thoughts About Death
W. O. Vaught, Jr.

The study of death and dying has revived in recent years as a subject for scientists and psychologists. Even in high school and college classrooms, some young people are taught how to make the necessary arrangements in the event someone close to them dies.

Past generations, with far shorter life expectancies, kept the subject out in the open almost to the point of obsession. And theologians were considered the authorities. From this, the pendulum swung to the opposite extreme and the mention of death became virtually taboo, not only in polite society but also on the street and in the home.

Within the last decade, concern with death and the afterlife has reasserted itself in many different guises, especially preoccupation with the occult. We need to go back to the Bible and search out what it has to say on the subject of death.

The Realities of Death

Let us look first at the Bible's explanation of the opposite of death—*physical life.*

A believer in the Lord Jesus Christ is said to be trichotomous, a three-part being, a being of body, soul, and spirit. The *soul* is the ability to understand and categorize things in the realm of physical phenomena; the *spirit* is the ability to understand and categorize things in the realm of spiritual phenomena.

When the believer dies, his soul and spirit, the real person, is removed into the presence of the Lord. The soul and spirit having left the body, it is placed in the grave. Too often, I believe, we make overmuch of the physical body after death. This, of course, is the pattern of heathenism, from the pyramids of Egypt to the burial platforms of the American Indians.

Let us go back for a moment and look at the cross of Christ, the instrument of his death. When we believe in Christ, we receive salvation, which is perfect and will never be improved. At that time, we begin to learn and apply Bible doctrine to our lives. The most important Bible truth we can grasp is that, having died with Christ, we will surely be resurrected with him.

The apostle John wrote, "Beloved, now are we the sons of God, and it doth not yet appear what we shall be: but we know that, when he shall appear, we shall be like him; for we shall see him as he is" (1 John 3:2). What cause for rejoicing!

According to 1 Thessalonians 4, at the end of the church age there will be a resurrection of believers: "even so them also who sleep in Jesus will God bring with him . . . and the dead in Christ shall rise first: then we which are alive and remain shall be caught up together with them" (vv. 14,16–17). Paul added, "Wherefore, comfort one another with these words" (v. 18).

In other places, also, the apostle Paul made much of this hope in Christ: "Who shall change our vile body, that it may be fashioned like unto his glorious body, according to the working whereby he is able even to subdue all things unto himself" (Phil. 3:21). This says that the *resurrection body* of the believer will be a body like that of the Son of God. It will preserve our personal identity, but it will have the perfection of Christ. The soul and spirit will occupy the resurrected body for all eternity.

This our new and glorified body will be able to travel in space; it will move readily through God's creation without any difficulty. This resurrected body cannot be harnessed in any way. It will not be affected by the destruction of the universe as we know it, which will come at the end of the millennium, or by the lake of fire.

The total history of the redeemed human personality will read like this: birth, life, death, soul and spirit with God, resurrection, perfection forever.

The transition from earth to heaven, from limitation to perfection, from sin and sorrow to permanent joy, hinges on the pivot of death. It is the portal which swings between them. To move from the impotence of this life into the flowering of eternal life, we must pass the gate of death—unless we should be among those in the generation during whose lifetime Christ comes to catch his own away.

The Usage of the Word Death

Physical Death

Every time we read the word *death* in the Bible, it does not necessarily refer to physical death. Of course, most of the time it does. In the Old Testament, each "begat" is followed by "and he died."

"All flesh is grass," wrote Isaiah, "and all its beauty is like the flower of the field. /The grass withers, the flower fades, /when the breath of the Lord blows upon it" (40:6–7, RSV). "Man that is born of a woman is of few days, and full of trouble," said Job. "He cometh forth like a flower, and is cut down: he fleeth also as a shadow, and continueth not" (14:1–2).

David, mourning the death of his infant son, said, "But now he is dead, . . . can I bring him back again? I shall go to him, but he shall not return to me" (2 Sam. 12:23).

In John 11:25, "Jesus said unto her [Martha], I am the resurrection, and the life: he that believeth in me, though he were dead, yet shall he live." And Paul wrote, "For to me to live is Christ, and to die is gain" (Phil. 1:21).

In Matthew 8:22 we read, "Let the dead [spiritially dead] bury their dead [physically dead]." The Christian should not be preoccupied with death, but with life.

Another kind of physical death, sexual death, was illustrated in the life story of Abraham and Sarah. Although they were dead sexually, in that their bodies were beyond having children, God revived them and made it possible for them to have a son.

"Through faith also," we read in Hebrews 11:11, "Sara herself received strength to conceive seed, and was delivered of a child when she was past age." Then of Abraham verse 12 says, "Therefore sprang there even of one, and him as good as dead, so many as the stars of the sky in multitude, and as the sand which is by the sea shore innumerable."

Sometimes the word *death* is used in reference to the Christian while he is still physically alive. One aspect is called *positional death*.

Once we are saved, we share Christ and all that he has. We are identified with him in his death. Jesus Christ was virgin-born, which means he did not have an old sin nature. Therefore he was able to bear the sins of every man in the whole human race—he was qualified to carry our sins, for he had none of his own. Because he died for us, we are identified with him in his death.

This is explained in detail by the apostle Paul in Romans 6:1–14. Some familiar verses often used in baptismal services contain the statement, "we are buried with him by baptism into death" (v. 4). Because of this, we are to "reckon . . . yourselves to be dead indeed unto sin, but alive unto God through Jesus Christ our Lord," and to "yield yourselves unto God, as those that are alive from the dead" (vv. 11,13). Paul summed it up with, "For sin shall not have dominion over you: for ye are not under the law, but under grace" (v. 14).

Paul discussed the subject again in Colossians saying that we are "buried with him in baptism, wherein also ye are risen with him through the faith of the operation of God, who hath raised him from the dead" (2:12). We actually died to sin at the cross. This is what we call *retroactive positional truth*.

Also, there is such a thing as *carnal death*. When a believer is out of fellowship with God, he is called "carnal."

"For to be carnally minded is death," Paul wrote, "but to be spiritually minded is life and peace" (Rom. 8:6). In verse 13 he said, "For if ye live after the flesh, ye shall die: but if ye through the Spirit do mortify the deeds of the body, ye shall live."

If we substitute, for the word *death* in these verses, "separation from God," we find it clarifies them: "to be carnally minded is separation from God," and "if ye live after the flesh, ye shall be separated from God."

Something very closely akin to carnal death is more accurately labeled *temporal death*.

We read in 1 Timothy 5:6, "But she that liveth in pleasure is dead while she liveth." And in James 1:15, "Then when lust hath conceived, it bringeth forth sin: and sin, when it is finished, bringeth forth death."

Christ instructed, in Revelation 3:1, "And unto the angel of the church in Sardis write; These things saith he that hath the seven Spirits of God, and the seven stars; I know thy works, that thou hast a name that thou livest, and art dead."

We find this temporal death illustrated in a familiar passage—the parable of the prodigal son. The father said, "For this my son was dead, and is alive again; he was lost, and is found." Later, the father said to the older brother, "this thy brother was dead, and is alive again; and was lost, and is found" (Luke 15:24,32).

Notice the record says, "This my *son* was dead and is alive again." Even when the young man was in a far country, however, he was still his father's son.

Spiritual Death

We are born in a condition of *spiritual death:* "And you hath he [Christ] quickened," we read in Ephesians 2:1, "who were dead in trespasses and sins."

In Romans, the apostle Paul spelled it out: "Wherefore, as by one man sin entered into the world, and death by sin; and so death passed upon all men, for that all have sinned" (5:12) and, "For the wages of sin is death; but the gift of God is eternal life through Jesus Christ our Lord" (6:23).

The barrier raised between man and God by sin is spiritual death. Man is born in sin; he is born spiritually dead. In Isaiah 53:9, we read a prophecy concerning Christ: "And he made his grave with the wicked, and with the rich in his death; because he had done no violence, neither was any deceit in his mouth."

In the Hebrew language, it reads, "in his deaths." On the cross, Jesus died twice. He died spiritually; then he died physically. At noon he cried out, "My God, my God, why hast thou forsaken me?" This was the time when he bore our sins and died spiritually for us.

Later, about three o'clock in the afternoon, he said, "It is finished," and he died physically. His spiritual death meant that our salvation was complete. His physical death meant that his work was done and that he was through with his earthly mission. To us, this means that since Christ died twice, man can be born twice. But if a man is born only once, then he will die twice.

The Second Death

The *second death* is the death of the unbeliever; it will be pronounced at the final judgment.

"And I saw the dead, small and great, stand before God," wrote John from Patmos, "and the books were opened: and another book was opened, which is the book of life: and the dead were judged out of those things which were written in the books, according to their works" (Rev. 20:12).

Notice that it is "the books," plural, in which their works were written, not the Book of Life. Verse 15 tells us, "And whosoever was not found written in the book of life was cast into the lake of fire."

These dead were evidently in some sort of resurrection bodies, for "the sea gave up the dead which were in it; and death and hell delivered up the dead which were in them: . . . And death and hell were cast into the lake of fire. This is the second death" (Rev. 20:13–14).

The Division of Humanity

In John 3:36, we have a statement made by Christ which divides humanity. "He that believeth on the Son hath everlasting life," Jesus said, "and he that believeth not the Son shall not see life; but the wrath of God abideth on him." This division is already a reality in each human life and will be extended throughout eternity.

"It is appointed unto men once to die, but after this the judgment," said the writer to the Hebrews (9:27).

When the Unbeliever Dies

The unbeliever is not trichotomous, like the believer. He is a dichotomous being—he has only a soul and a body.

At death, the soul of the unbeliever leaves the body and goes to hades, a temporary place of suffering, as we learn from the story of the rich man and Lazarus.

At the resurrection of the unjust, the soul is reunited with the body. "But the rest of the dead lived not again," we read in Revelation 20:5, "until the thousand years were finished. This is the [rest of the] first resurrection." In later verses of the same chapter the scene of judgment is described in detail, ending, "This is the second death. And whosoever was not found written in the book of life was cast into the lake of fire" (Rev. 20:14–15).

And in 21:27, "And there shall in no wise enter into it [the holy city, new Jerusalem] anything that defileth, . . . but they which are written in the Lamb's book of life."

Please notice that *sin* is not the issue in the judgment of unbelievers. The issue is good works: they trusted in their good works, but good works, no matter how many or how great, are never adequate. The unbeliever, not found "written in the Lamb's book of life" (Rev. 21:27), is cast into the lake of fire forever.

When the Believer Dies

The believer, when he dies, will never have an appointment with judgment. "There is therefore now no condemnation to them which are in Christ Jesus," we read in Romans 8:1, "who walk not after the flesh, but after the Spirit." Judgment is for the unbeliever, not the believer.

In 1 Corinthians 3:11–16 there is a reference to the fact that the believer's works will be tried by fire. The gold and silver and precious stones will abide. The hay, wood, and stubble—the deeds of our old sin nature—will be burned up. Remember, God burns up everything we accomplish by our own human effort. But all that we accomplish in the power of the Spirit will abide forever. The things burned are the things we did in the energy of the flesh.

At death, the believer is face to face with God. "We are confident," said Paul in 2 Corinthians 5:8, "and willing rather to be absent from the body, and to be present with the Lord." The Greek word for "present" means "face to face" with the Lord.

We will never have any regrets in heaven. "God shall wipe away all tears from their eyes," John said in Revelation 21:4, "and there shall be no more death, neither sorrow, nor crying, neither shall there be any more pain: for the former things are passed away."

We will have an abiding inheritance and an incorruptible crown: "every man that striveth for the mastery is temperate in all things. Now they do it to obtain a corruptible crown; but we an incorruptible" (1 Cor. 9:25).

Death, for the believer, involves only a move to a new and better home. "Let not your heart be troubled," Jesus told his disciples who were reacting to his announcement that he was going to leave them. "I go to prepare a place for you. And if I go and prepare a place for you, I will come again, and receive you unto myself; that where I am, there ye may be also" (John 14:1–3).

Most of all, death will give us a full realization of the magnificence of eternal life. Here, no one can fully understand what it will be like—not until we get to heaven and can experience it.

The Prospect of Dying Grace

In view of all that lies beyond death for the believer, we should not fear it. Having guided and blessed us throughout life, God will not forsake us then. "Precious in the sight of the Lord is the death of his saints" (Ps. 116:15).

As we approach the end of life, we move into what the Bible calls *dying grace*. Many of us have had relatives or friends to die very suddenly. One moment they were alive and the next moment, without any warning, they were rushed into eternity. However, the majority of individuals do not die in this way. Time is involved and death comes slowly or gradually. In both instances, God provides dying grace for every single one of his children.

Take an illustration of one who died very suddenly. About them, we so often say: "Just yesterday he (or she) was so happy and so alive. It's hard to believe that today he (or she) is dead." This was God's gift of life and happiness and blessing just before death. This was dying grace.

But if one suffers a long illness, or if death doesn't come so suddenly, we find that God provides for his own a period of stability, happiness, contentment, and it often turns out that they witness to their families and friends of the great grace and glory of God. Those of us who have watched illness and death in the lives of believers have seen this very thing enacted again and again.

As John Wesley said, "Our people die well." He meant that there is a difference between the death of the believer and of the unbeliever. The believer always has dying grace.

David did not fear death. "Yea, though I walk through the valley of the shadow of death, I will fear no evil," he sang, "for thou art with me; thy rod and thy staff, they comfort me" (Ps. 23:4). That statement, "I will fear no *evil*," refers to death. In other words, "I will not be afraid of death."

If you fear death, if you avoid certain things such as flying in a plane or riding in a car because you fear the consequences, then this Scripture is for you. There is nothing in the Bible that says we should be afraid of death. Rather, it always says we are not to fear death, for if we are in Christ, when we come to die, we will be given dying grace.

There is an amazing passage on this subject in the book of Job. Notice the teaching of some of these verses: "Behold, happy is the man whom God correcteth: therefore despise not thou the chastening of the Almighty. He shall deliver thee in six troubles: yea, in seven there shall no evil touch thee" (5:17,19). In all our troubles, even in death, God delivers his own.

"Thou shalt be hid from the scourge of the tongue," the passage continues, "neither shalt thou be afraid of destruction when it cometh" (vv. 21–22). The words, "be afraid of destruction," mean that we are not to fear death. "For thou shalt be in league with the stones of the field: and the beasts of the field shall be at peace with thee" (5:23). This means that the dangers of life cannot touch you until God is ready to take you.

Your temporary house will pass away, but you can have peace in your mind: "And thou shalt know that thy tabernacle shall be in peace; and thou shalt visit thy habitation, and shalt not sin" (5:24). When you die, you move into a new home where no sin can ever touch you—you cannot sin. This is the doctrine of ultimate sanctification.

"Thou shalt come to thy grave in a full age, like as a shock of corn cometh in in his season" (5:26). This means that when you are mature, whether you be a baby, a youth, or an aged person—if you are mature in God's sight and it is your time to go—then you will have dying grace. "Lo, this, we have searched it, so it is; hear it, and know thou it for thy good" (5:27).

You can actually laugh at death and not be afraid at all. You can look at death, and because you know doctrine, you are not the least bit afraid. With Paul, you can say to death, "O death, where is thy sting? O grave, where is thy victory?" (1 Cor. 15:55).

Contributing Authors

R. Earl Allen is pastor of Rosen Heights Baptist Church, Fort Worth, Texas.

Carl E. Bates is pastor of First Baptist Church, Charlotte, North Carolina, and a past president of the Southern Baptist Convention.

R. Y. Bradford is executive director of the Baptist Convention of New Mexico.

James W. Bryant is pastor of Sagamore Hill Baptist Church, Fort Worth, Texas.

Russell H. Dilday, Jr. is pastor of Ponce-De-Leon Baptist Church, Atlanta, Georgia, and past chairman of the Home Mission Board of the Southern Baptist Convention.

Carl Duck is pastor of Lakeside Baptist Church, Dallas, Texas.

David James Farmer is associate chaplain at Baptist Hospital, Nashville, Tennessee.

Charles G. Fuller is pastor of First Baptist Church, Roanoke, Virginia.

Charles E. Harvey is pastor of Sunset Acres Baptist Church, Shreveport, Louisiana, and past chairman of the Executive Committee, Southern Baptist Convention.

Herschel H. Hobbs is pastor emeritus of First Baptist Church, Oklahoma City, Oklahoma, and a past president of the Southern Baptist Convention.

Richard Jackson is pastor of North Phoenix Baptist Church, Phoenix, Arizona, and president of the Arizona Baptist Convention.

Landrum Leavell is president of the New Orleans Baptist Seminary, New Orleans, Louisiana.

W. Randall Lolley is president of Southeastern Baptist Seminary, Wake Forest, North Carolina.

Jack P. Lowndes is executive secretary of the Baptist Convention of New York and is a past president of the Home Mission Board of the Southern Baptist Convention.

Wesley R. Monfalcone is chaplain and director of the Clinical Pastoral Education Program at Louisville General Hospital, Louisville, Kentucky.

Walter G. Nunn is pastor of First Baptist Church, Jasper, Alabama.

James L. Pleitz is pastor of Park Cities Baptist Church, Dallas, Texas, and a past president of the Pastor's Conference of the Southern Baptist Convention.

Francis Jackson Redford is director of the Extension Department of the Home Mission Board, Southern Baptist Convention, and a Major (Chaplain), U. S. Army (retired).

Mahan Siler, Jr., Department of Pastoral Care, North Carolina Baptist Hospitals, Inc., Winston-Salem, North Carolina.

W. Ches Smith, III, is pastor of First Baptist Church, Tifton, Georgia, and chairman of the Executive Committee of the Southern Baptist Convention.

Jaroy Weber is pastor of First Baptist Church, Lubbock, Texas, and a past president of the Southern Baptist Convention.

James P. Wesberry is pastor emeritus of Morningside Baptist Church, Atlanta, Georgia; executive director of The Lord's Day Alliance of the United States; and editor of *Sunday* magazine.

W. O. Vaught is pastor of Immanuel Baptist Church, Little Rock, Arkansas, a past president of the Arkansas Baptist Convention, and a past president of the Pastor's Conference of the Southern Baptist Convention.